How To Train Your Spouse

Creating the Marriage You Desire by Becoming
the Spouse God Has Called You to Be

Amber Cunningham

WESTBOW
PRESS°
A DIVISION OF THOMAS NELSON
& ZONDERVAN

WestBow Press books may be ordered through booksellers or by contacting:

WestBow Press
A Division of Thomas Nelson & Zondervan
1663 Liberty Drive
Bloomington, IN 47403
www.westbowpress.com
844-714-3454

ISBN: 979-8-3850-3445-1 (sc)
ISBN: 979-8-3850-3446-8 (e)

Library of Congress Control Number: 2024920752

Print information available on the last page.

WestBow Press rev. date: 10/08/2024

CONTENTS

ACKNOWLEDGMENTS

To my God, who saved, redeemed, healed, and continues to mold me into the person He desires me to be. I cannot thank You enough for all that You have done in my life, marriage, and family. I love You with all of my heart and will serve You all the days of my life. Thank You, Lord, for Your guidance and words in writing this book. May You be glorified!

To my husband, Eric, for becoming the godly husband that I always dreamed of sharing my life with and the godly father that our children need. God knew that I needed *you*! I am so blessed to have you by my side and so thankful for the life that we have built together. You are my biggest supporter, and you love me so well. Love you always and forever!

To all of my children and grandchildren, my greatest blessings call me, *Mom* and *Gigi.* I am so proud of you all and love you so much! I pray that you will love the Lord all the days of your life and will serve the purposes of God in your generation. I pray for all of your marriages and what God joins together, let no man separate (Mark 10:9).

To my dad, Randy Jones, in whose memory this book was written, who always jokingly said that he knew how to train a woman and that he should write a book about it someday. Who knew that his joke would be an inspiration for my first book title. Dad, you were one of a kind! I love and miss you.

To my mom, Deb, for being my biggest prayer warrior and cheerleader. Thank you for always loving me and supporting me in whatever I do. You are a blessing. Love you!

To my stepdad, Rick, for always being there for me and showing me the Father's love. I thank God that He brought you into my life. Love you!

To my spiritual mentor and friend, Katherine, for teaching, encouraging, and challenging me even when I did not want to be challenged. I could not have written this book without your wisdom and prayers. You were a godsend many years ago!

PRAYER FOR MARRIAGES

Heavenly Father, I pray for every person who will read this book. We know that it is not by chance that they have this book in their hands right now. God, I pray for open hearts and minds to receive what You want them to receive. Open their eyes to see what You want them to see, and open their ears to hear what the Spirit of God is saying. Lord, help them to take away the truths and apply them to their own marriage. I pray that they would put You first in their lives and watch You transform their marriage into what You want it to be. Strengthen, heal, restore, and work in every marriage. We know that nothing is impossible for You. Turn hearts to You, Jesus. Touch every marriage and make it into something beautiful for Your glory in Jesus's name. Amen.

INTRODUCTION

I was young and in love with my dream guy, whom I had a crush on ever since I was in grade school. We started dating when I was sixteen years old and he was twenty. We had our firstborn son, out of wedlock, at the ages of seventeen and twenty-one, and we were later married when we were just twenty and twenty-four years young. We did everything backward. We had no clue what a marriage was to look like. We went into it blindly, just two kids who fell in love and thought it would be pure bliss like the movies portrayed it to be.

Nobody told us that marriage would be hard, that it would take constant work, and that it would take dying to our selfish nature daily. No one told us the truth that love is a choice, not just a feeling, and that the butterflies would soon fade away.

We made our vows on our wedding day, June 23, 2001. We vowed to love one another and stay together in the good times and the bad, in sickness and in health, until death do us part. We got pregnant with our second son right after we married. Everything seemed great while we were still in the honeymoon stage, but then, life happened. Financial troubles arose, and sicknesses came. Our second son was born with congenital hypothyroidism and was sick for the first three years of his life. We did not know how to deal with the stress of a sick baby. I was depressed and had no idea how to manage being a wife and a mom. We found ourselves using the big *D* word as troubles arose. It seemed easier to just quit rather than fight all the time.

It was not until the stress started to take its toll on our own bodies that we finally had our wake-up call. What goes on inside of us will always find a way to manifest on the outside of us. My husband developed shingles several times, which would break out on his face. I developed inflammatory arthritis in both my feet and ankles at the age of twenty-six, which debilitated me for over a year. I could hardly walk. Every morning, I would crawl out of bed and scoot down the stairs on my bottom to go take my medicine in the kitchen. After the medicine finally kicked in, I could use the counter to pull myself up to my feet. It was the most pain that I have ever experienced in my life, and I have had five C-sections. I thought I had a high pain tolerance until I experienced that pain.

I started seeing a rheumatologist, who prescribed me high doses of steroids and anti-inflammatory medication, as well as administered injections in my feet and ankles. I tested positive for a gene called HLA-B27, which causes ankylosing spondylitis, a crippling arthritis of the spine.

We hit rock bottom in our marriage and did not know where to turn. Our last resort was to turn to God and give the church a try. I believe that God allowed me to be knocked off my feet so I would look up to Him.

> Sometimes God lets you hit rock bottom so you will discover that He is the rock at the bottom.
>
> —Tony Evans

We gave our lives to Christ and decided to turn things around for our family. My husband and I started praying together and went to two different churches, one on Saturday evening and another on Sunday morning. Things started to look up for us. We saw God begin to work in our lives and in our marriage. As the arthritis began to move to my spine, we prayed for healing and for a miracle in my body. I completely surrendered to God and to His will. I told Him that I would live for Him for the rest of my life and do whatever He asked me to do. *Just please heal me and take the arthritis pain away.*

I felt the Lord was telling me to have another child. I thought, *I don't know how I can have another child when I can hardly take care of the two children that I have since I can barely walk.* The very next day, I went to see my rheumatologist. He told me he could not keep me on steroids and anti-inflammatory medications any longer since I had been on them for an entire year. He said he needed to put me on a stronger medication, one that they put rheumatoid arthritis patients on. But he asked me whether I would like to have more children. I told him that we did want to have more children but not right away. He told me that I could not get pregnant if I were on the new medication and that I would need to be off it for six months before I could get pregnant due to its side effects, which could harm the baby. He then told me that this type of arthritis had been put in remission with pregnancy, so he prescribed me to *get pregnant.*

It was a total God moment! The Lord had just put on my heart the night before to have another child, and then my doctor prescribed that I get pregnant. Well, we got pregnant by the next month, and I never went back to see my rheumatologist again. All the pain in my feet, ankles, and back was immediately gone! God had answered my prayer and completely healed my body with my pregnancy of our third child—our beautiful baby girl. Not only did He bring healing to my body, but He also began to bring healing to my marriage. Glory to God!

That moment was the turning point in my relationship with Christ. I had made the decision to surrender to Him and make Him Lord over my life. He in turn brought healing to my body and to my marriage. I have kept my promise and, to this day, continue to love and serve the Lord wholeheartedly, doing whatever He asks me to do. Now, seventeen years later, I can look back and see all the amazing things that God has done in and through me, my marriage, our family, and our ministry. He is so good and faithful!

God put on my heart to write this book. At first, I was hesitant. I have never written a book, nor do I know anything about publishing one. I certainly did not want to write about marriage because I knew from experience that whatever you teach, you will be tested on and will have to walk through yourself. I was comfortable and did not want to be tested. I was quickly reminded that we do not grow in our comfort zones; we grow when we are tested and challenged. God is taking us to another level in our marriage, and He wants us to help other married couples do the same. I said yes to God. After all, when you make a promise to God, you keep your promises. My husband and I are passionate about marriage and family. We want to share what we have learned and help as many people as possible.

As we celebrated twenty-three years of marriage this year, I can look back and see all that God has taught us and is still teaching us. We want to share with you twenty-three marriage tips and how we learned to train our spouse, from submission and giving up control to affirming and honoring. We invite you to take this journey with us. Learn from our mistakes and find ways to make your marriage grow stronger and better than ever before. Trust me, it will be worth it!

CHAPTER 1

How to Train Your Spouse

Wives, be subject to your own husbands, as [a service] to the LORD. For the husband is head of the wife, as Christ is head of the church, Himself being the Savior of the body. But as the church is subject to Christ, so also wives should be subject to their husbands in everything [respecting both their position as protector and their responsibility to God as head of the house]. Husbands, love your wives [seek the highest good for her and surround her with a caring, unselfish love], just as Christ also loved the church and gave Himself up for her.

—Ephesians 5:22–25 (AMP)

I had it all figured out—or so I thought I did. We were so in love, and I had my man wrapped around my little finger. We got married at the young ages of twenty and twenty-four years old. It was exciting! It was going to be such bliss.

No one told me that the honeymoon phase would soon end. No one told me that we would irritate each other and that our differences would become an annoyance. No one told me that he would do things that were completely the opposite of the way that I do things. No one told me that marriage was hard and that it required daily attention.

It was my way or the highway. I could control him by throwing fits or giving him the silent treatment. I thought nagging would help change my husband. I thought that if I complained, harped on him, or controlled him long enough it would change him into the man *I* thought he should be. Was I ever wrong!

I was miserable, and I learned that miserable people make others miserable. Misery loves company. I was worn out and frustrated, and it seemed that we kept going around the same mountain over and over. Like Dr. Phil always asks, "How's that working for you?" Let me tell you, it was not! It wasn't until God started to deal with me in regard to my marriage that things began to change.

We decided to attend a marriage conference. While we were there, I felt led to ask one of the speakers if she would mentor and help me. She agreed to meet with me once a week. I was a mess. I had all these different issues going on in my life, and I remember her saying that we were going to tackle my marriage first. I thought that we should be dealing with the financial issues, my business, parenting, or something else, but she assured me that my marriage was the first place to start because everything would flow from that. I hated to admit it, but she was right.

I was excited to start meeting with her so she could agree with me about all the things that my husband was doing wrong. I thought that it would be so good to have someone to talk to and for her to affirm that what I was doing was right. She could help me change him. Once again, I was proven wrong.

Everything I shared with her, she would respond by asking me how I handled it and why it bothered me. She would ask me what the root of the problem was. I wanted to say, "I don't know. You tell me." She would constantly take my pointing finger and point it back to me to see what my part was and what I was doing wrong. My flesh did not like it one bit. I was thinking, *She is not helping me at all. All she is doing is blaming me.* But God was teaching me through her to die to my selfish nature and to look within at my own heart. Marriage is not about making us happy; marriage is about making us more holy.

> Pride must die in you, or nothing of heaven can live in you.
> —Andrew Murray

Our selfish nature wants to point fingers and find fault in others. It wants to put the blame on someone else rather than have us look within and be accountable for our own actions.

> And why do you look at the speck in your brother's eye, but do not consider the plank in your own eye? Or how can you say to your brother, 'Let me remove the speck from your eye'; and look, a plank is in your own eye? Hypocrite! First remove the plank from your own eye, and then you will see clearly to remove the speck from your brother's eye. (Matthew 7:3–5 NKJV)

I found out that I had a lot of pride. At first, I thought, *Pride? I don't have pride.* Well, I soon learned that those who think they don't have pride are filled with pride. Pride says, "I know it all." Pride says, "My way is the best way." Pride says, "You are wrong, and I am right." Pride says, "I can feel sorry for myself, pout, and throw a fit." Pride says, "I need to have the last word or do all the talking." Pride does not like to admit when it is wrong. Pride is ugly. Pride is hard to love. Pride is destructive, and it destroys relationships.

It seemed as though every issue that came up when I met with my mentor would come back to either pride or fear. Like it or not, we all struggle with pride. It is part of our selfish nature, but it can be dealt with as God teaches us how to walk in humility each day. My prideful nature made me very selfish, and it was all about me. I had to constantly repent to God for being prideful and ask Him to humble me.

Satan fell because of pride. Pride always goes before the fall. God's Word says in James 4:6 (NLT), "God opposes the proud but gives grace to the humble." Proverbs 29:23 (CSB) says, "A person's pride will humble him, but a humble spirit will gain honor."

I learned that even if I was only 1 percent wrong, I had to own up to my part. Wow, was that humbling. It seemed as though I was constantly repenting. This was so hard for me at first. Pride does not like to admit or apologize when it is wrong. The humblest person is the one who repents first. Well, in my case, it was not me who was apologizing first; it was always my husband. After he said sorry, then I could finally say those two dreaded words because he admitted it first. I also learned that there is a big difference between merely apologizing and actually repenting. You can apologize a million times for the same thing because you are stuck in a cycle of repeating the same offense. You can apologize and be forgiven each time you do something, but to repent means that you are deciding to change your ways and not commit that offense again.

The Greek term for repentance, *metanoia*, means to change one's mind. If we do not truly repent and change our minds about the way that we are acting, then we will just continue to act the same way, thus going around the same mountain over and over. I learned that repenting meant being truly sorrowful for what I had done, humbling myself to admit that I was wrong, and asking for forgiveness. Sorrow for our sins will result in changed behavior. Many people are sorry only for the effects of their sins or for being caught. This is sorrow "which lacks repentance."

Second Corinthians 7:10 (NIV) says, "Godly sorrow brings repentance that leads to salvation and leaves no regret, but worldly sorrow brings death." Worldly grief is what Judas experienced after he betrayed Jesus. He knew he had sinned and was filled with remorse, but he was unwilling to repent to God. Peter, on the other hand, experienced godly grief after denying Christ three times. This led to his repentance and recommitment to the Lord, resulting in his spiritual restoration. Both denied Christ. One repented and was restored to faith and service; the other one took his own life.

I can now honestly say that I am quick to repent as soon as the Lord convicts me of something I have said or done. I want to please the Lord, so I am quick to obey when He convicts me of my wrongs.

Pride is concerned with who is right. Humility is concerned with what is right.

—Ezra Taft Benson

Do nothing from selfishness or empty conceit [through factional motives, or strife], but with [an attitude of] humility [being neither arrogant nor self-righteous], regard others as more important than yourselves. Do not merely look out for your own personal interests, but also for the interests of others. (Philippians 2:3–4 AMP)

It was not just pride I was dealing with. I had a ton of fear in my life. My controlling nature came from a root of fear. The more we fear, the more we will try to control. Whatever we fear the most actually reveals where we trust God the least. The spirit of fear causes us to control while the fear of the Lord results in surrender and obedience. If you find a controlling person, most likely they have a lot of fear in their life. The Bible tells us that fear is a spirit, and if you allow it to, it will control you. The good news is that if you are a born-again believer and have accepted Christ into your life, then Jesus has given you authority over this spirit of fear.

In Luke 10:19, Jesus says that He has given us authority to trample on serpents and scorpions and over all the power of the enemy, and nothing shall, by any means, hurt us. Jesus gave us authority over the enemy, but most people do not know how to use it. The Bible says, "Therefore submit to God, resist the devil, and he will flee from you" (James 4:7 NKJV). We must resist and rebuke the enemy. Whenever you feel fear trying to dominate your mind, you resist it in the name of Jesus. Second Timothy 1:7 (NKJV) says, "For God has not given us a spirit of fear, but of power and of love and of a sound mind." In 1 John 4:18 it says, "There is no fear in love; but perfect love casts out fear, because fear involves torment. But he who fears has not been made perfect in love." The more we experience God's love in our lives, the less we will fear.

When Jesus was led into the wilderness by the Holy Spirit to fast for forty days and forty nights, Satan came to tempt him three times (see Matthew 4 and Luke 4). Each time, Jesus responded to his temptation, "It is written …, It is written …, It is written." Jesus overcame the enemy with the Word of God. Your biggest weapon against Satan's schemes is God's Word. It is your sword (see Ephesians 6:17). Satan is allergic to scripture. Find scriptures that you can meditate on and use whenever the enemy comes to attack. Do not allow the enemy to control you anymore with fear and anxiety. Use the authority that Jesus gave you and rebuke the spirit of fear in Jesus's name. Surrender your cares and concerns to the Lord and trust that He will take care of whatever concerns you. Remember, if we are trying to control a person or situation, it reveals that we are not trusting God in that area of our lives.

> Behold, I give you the authority to trample on serpents and scorpions, and over all the power of the enemy, and nothing shall by any means hurt you. (Luke 10:19 NKJV)

> For God did not give us a spirit of timidity or cowardice or fear, but [He has given us a spirit] of power and of love and of sound judgment and personal discipline [abilities that result in a calm, well-balanced mind, and self-control]. (2 Timothy 1:7 AMP)

> There is no fear in love; but perfect love casts out fear, because fear involves torment. But he who fears has not been made perfect in love. (1 John 4:18 NKJV)

> Casting all your cares [all your anxieties, all your worries, and all your concerns, once and for all] on Him, for He cares about you [with deepest affection, and watches over you very carefully]. (1 Peter 5:7 AMP)

If you want to have a successful marriage, then you must surrender to God and do things His way. Early on in our marriage, I thought that I was in control, the head of our home, and that I ruled the roost. But according to Ephesians 5:22–23, wives are to submit to their husbands, as to the Lord. For the husband is the head of the wife, as also Christ is the head of the church. The husband is to be the head of the home. Well, maybe that was the case for some men, but my husband wasn't the *leading* type. He just went with the flow and was a people pleaser, so he did whatever I wanted.

Whenever I asked him to lead, he did not know how. He was passive. My type-A personality and his passiveness were the best combination for our home to be out of order. He didn't know how to step up and lead; I didn't know how to take a step back and encourage him to do so. We needed help.

It took a lot of prayer and mentorship for us to figure it out. My mentor kept telling me that I was out of position and that everything flowed from the top. When we are out of order in our positions with God and our marriage, then everything else is going to be affected. Anytime that we are out of position in our homes, there is going to be chaos and disorder. God is a God of order. He is head over us, and our husbands are to be head of the home. But the problem was I still did not know how to do it, or even what that looked like. We had functioned like that our whole marriage and had never seen anything else modeled to us. Lord, help!

The Lord started to teach me about honor. The definition of honor is "high respect" and "great esteem." I needed to start by respecting my husband. What is respect? Respect is a feeling of deep admiration for someone elicited by their abilities, qualities, or achievements. It is also due regard for the feelings, wishes, rights, or traditions of others. What that meant was that I needed to honor my husband by esteeming him, admiring him, giving him my time and attention, and valuing his opinions and wishes. I started asking him what he wanted instead of always doing what I wanted. I asked him where he wanted to go and eat. However, he would always respond with, "I don't care ... whatever you want." But at least I asked. I valued what he said.

As we were getting our finances in order, I started asking permission for anything I wanted to buy. If he did not approve of it, I would respect that. I remember one day having some clothing for our girls in our Walmart cart and standing in the checkout line as I remembered that I should ask him for his approval. I figured that he would say yes, as he always appreciated that I took the time to ask. Well, in this instance, and for the very first time, he said the dreaded word: "No." I struggled at first. I didn't want to put the clothes back, but I humbled myself and did it anyway. When we honor one another, we honor the Lord.

Besides asking my husband for his thoughts/opinions and valuing his answers, I started encouraging him. I learned that saying, "You need to step up," does *not* work, but encouragement does. I started encouraging my husband for the smallest of things. I remember my mentor telling me to even thank him every time he takes out the trash or does anything around the house. At first I thought, *Well, I don't get a thank-you for all the things that I do around the house.* It was as if my mentor could read my mind because she reminded me that it was *not* about me; it was about honoring my husband and doing my part to encourage him. She said, "Even if the only good thing he does is get out of bed in the morning, encourage him for that."

Man, was this hard at first. It seemed as though I could encourage everyone else but him. I started by thanking him for the little things, as hard as it was for the words to come out of my mouth. But then I found that the more I appreciated and encouraged him, the more he helped around the house and the better man he became. He started to rise to be the man that I had wanted him to be. People rise when they are lifted, not when they are being beaten down. Was that really all it took was to humble myself and honor and affirm him? Why did my flesh fight it so hard?

> Behind every great man is a great woman.
>
> —Proverb

> A man's success has a lot to do with the kind of woman he chooses to have in his life. A great woman brings forward a great man.
>
> —Unknown

Have you ever seen a successful godly man who walks around with humble confidence and fulfills his God-given destiny? He did not get there on his own. It is because he has had great people around him, usually a great father or mother, grandfather or grandmother, or wife who prayed for him, encouraged him, spoke life over him, and helped him to become all that God created him to be.

On the contrary, have you ever been around a man with no confidence and witnessed him walking around like a dog with his tail between his legs? It is usually because he has been beaten down with negative words rather than built up with positive, life-giving compliments. When we build up our men instead of tearing them down, they will rise to be the men that God created them to be.

The wise woman builds her house [on a foundation of godly precepts, and her household thrives], but the foolish one [who lacks spiritual insight] tears it down with her own hands [by ignoring godly principles]. (Proverbs 14:1 AMP)

The same is true for the men. Husbands, you are to love your wives as Christ loved the Church (Ephesians 5:25). Jesus Christ loved us so much that He laid down His life for the church. Husbands, do you love your wives so much that you would lay down your lives for them? Would Jesus approve of the way that you talk to them or treat them? In Ephesians 5:25, the apostle Paul prohibits every attitude or behavior that results in a husband devaluing, humiliating, belittling, or emotionally or physically wounding his wife. Colossians 3:19 also commands husbands to love their wives and not be harsh with them. When a husband speaks down to his wife and is harsh with his words, he is not only dishonoring her, he is also dishonoring the Lord.

Our words can either speak life or speak death. Our tongues can build others up, or they can tear them down. Proverbs 18:21 (NIV) says, "The tongue has the power of life and death, and those who love it will eat its fruit." You will frame up your life with the words that you speak. If you want to see what direction your life or marriage is headed, just listen to the words that you are speaking. There is power in our words. Change your words, and you will change your life. Control your mouth, and you can control the direction of your life. Your tongue is like fire (see James 3). Your tongue can burn down your marriage, family, business, and your life. Be the husband and wife who bless each other with your words and help each other rise to be the people God created you to be.

I have learned that as I allow God to work in my own heart and change me, then He also does the work in my spouse. As I become the woman God has created me to be, He helps my husband to become who he was meant to be, and vice versa. It has been a journey of living and learning, being obedient to what God asks us to do, and extending lots of love and grace.

It is not about you trying to train and change your spouse; rather, it's about allowing God to make the changes that He needs to make in each one of you to make you the spouse that He wants you to be. There is no amount of human strength or willpower to try to change yourself, your spouse, or your marriage. We can only do it with God's help and the power of the Holy Spirit. When we stop trying to do it on our own and humbly surrender to God, His Word, and His process, then we will see the results that we desire to see. If God is not at the center of your life and marriage, then that is the first place to start. You will not have a healthy marriage apart from Him. Invite Jesus into your heart, into your life, and into your marriage. It will be the best decision that you will ever make. Come with us on this journey as we allow God to mold us, change us, and make our marriages more of a reflection of Him.

Summary

- Marriage is not about making *you* happy; marriage is about making you more holy.
- Pride is concerned with who is right. Humility is concerned with what is right.
- Whatever we fear the most reveals where we trust God the least.
- When we honor each other, we honor the Lord.
- Wives, you are to submit to your husband as to the Lord. Husbands, you are to love your wife as Christ loved the Church and gave Himself up for her (Ephesians 5:22–25).
- If you want to see what direction your life or marriage is headed, just listen to the words that you are speaking.
- We cannot change ourselves or our spouse by our own strength or willpower. We can only do it with God's help and the power of the Holy Spirit.

Questions

1. How is the Holy Spirit speaking to me through this chapter?

2. Husbands, are you loving your wife the way that God calls you to love? Wives, are you submitted to your husband and showing him respect? What can you do to show more love and respect to your spouse?

3. How is pride or fear affecting my marriage?

4. What needs to change in our marriage?

Prayer

Heavenly Father, I invite You into my heart and marriage. I know that I cannot change myself without Your help. You are the only One who can work within each of us. Help me to stop pointing the finger at my spouse and look within at myself. Show me any pride or fear that I have in my life. Change me and help me to become the man or woman that You have created me to be. I submit to You, God, and humbly ask for Your help with my marriage in Jesus's name. Amen.

CHAPTER 2

Alignment

But first and most importantly seek (aim at, strive after) His kingdom and His righteousness [His way of doing and being right—the attitude and character of God], and all these things will be given to you also.

—Matthew 6:33 (AMP)

To have a healthy marriage, which I believe we all genuinely want and desire, we must keep our lives in alignment. Does that mean we live perfect lives? Absolutely not. None of us are perfect, and we all sin and fall short of the glory of God (Romans 3:23). Jesus was the only perfect person to ever walk this earth. Since there are no perfect people other than Jesus, that means there is no such thing as a perfect marriage. My husband and I do not have a perfect marriage, but we do have a growing marriage—one that is centered in Christ.

Matthew 6:33 tells us that if we seek first the kingdom of God and His righteousness, then all these things shall be added to us. When we pursue God's kingdom and His righteousness as our priority for living, then God will take care of everything else in our lives.

If we look at the context of Matthew 6:33, we see in the previous verses (vv. 25–32) what the cure for anxiety is. These verses tell us to not worry about our lives or what we will eat, drink, or wear. God feeds the birds of the sky; aren't we worth more than them? Our Heavenly Father knows what we need before we ever ask Him. As we seek first God's Kingdom and His righteousness, then all the things that we need will be provided for us.

Do Not Worry

> Therefore I say to you, do not worry about your life, what you will eat or what you will drink; nor about your body, what you will put on. Is not life more than food and the body more than clothing? Look at the birds of the air, for they neither sow nor reap nor gather into barns; yet your heavenly Father feeds them. Are you not of more value than they? Which of you by worrying can add one cubit to his stature? So why do you worry about clothing? Consider the lilies of the field, how they grow: they neither toil nor spin; and yet I say to you that even Solomon in all his glory was not arrayed like one of these. Now if God so clothes the grass of the field, which today is, and tomorrow is thrown into the oven, will He not much more clothe you, O you of little faith? Therefore do not worry, saying, "What shall we eat?" or "What shall we drink?" or 'What shall we wear?" For after all these things the Gentiles seek. For your heavenly Father knows that you

need all these things. But seek first the kingdom of God and His righteousness, and all these things shall be added to you. Therefore do not worry about tomorrow, for tomorrow will worry about its own things. Sufficient for the day is its own trouble. (Matthew 6:25–34 NKJV)

As humans, we tend to strive to make everything happen on our own. It is such a freeing feeling when we put God first and allow Him to be our provider and take care of all our needs. God is a God of order. He wants to be number one in our lives. The first two of the Ten Commandments that God gave to Moses in Exodus 20:3–4 are (1) You shall have no other gods before me and (2) You shall not make for yourself an idol. When a Pharisee asked Jesus in Matthew 22:35–36 (NIV) what the greatest commandment in the law was, Jesus replied: "'Love the Lord your God with all your heart and with all your soul and with all your mind.' This is the first and greatest commandment. And the second is like it: 'Love your neighbor as yourself.' All the Law and the Prophets hang on these two commandments" (Matthew 22:37–40 NIV).

God makes it very clear that He desires for us to love Him and put Him first in our lives. But so often, we tend to let the busyness of life take over, and we end up putting everything else before Him, giving Him only our leftover time. When we do that, we will end up being burned out, frustrated, tired, weary, and bearing no fruit in our lives. John 15:5 (NIV) says, "I am the vine; you are the branches. If you remain in me and I in you, you will bear much fruit; apart from me you can do nothing."

It is simple. If we do not spend time with the God who created us, we will bear no fruit in our lives and can do nothing apart from Him. But when we connect ourselves to Him through worship, spending time in His presence, reading His Word and prayer, then we will bear the good fruit in our lives that we all desire. Galatians 5:22–23 (NLT) says, "But the Holy Spirit produces this kind of fruit in our lives: love, joy peace, patience, kindness, goodness, faithfulness, gentleness, and self-control. There is no law against these things!" If you are not producing these fruits in your life, it is time to reconnect with the Lord. Anytime that I am not walking in the fruit of the spirit, I give myself a spiritual timeout to go and spend time with God. We dry up so quickly and need to connect ourselves to Jesus all throughout the day. I know that

I cannot be the wife, mother, and person that I desire to be unless I spend time with Jesus every day. If we want to bear any fruit in our lives, we must stay connected to the Vine. When we abide in Him, we will bear much fruit!

Maybe you have put God first in your own life, but He's not first in your marriage. Or maybe you have a relationship with the Lord, but your spouse does not. What do you do? You *pray*! Prayer is what connects us to God, and it is our most powerful weapon. Nothing happens in our lives unless we pray. James 5:16 (AMP) says, "Therefore, confess your sins to one another [your false steps, your offenses], and pray for one another, that you may be healed and restored. The heartfelt and persistent prayer of a righteous man (believer) can accomplish much [when put into action and made effective by God—it is dynamic and can have tremendous power]."

There is so much power in a praying husband or wife. You may not see anything happening in the natural world, but keep praying and be persistent. God hears you and will answer your prayers in His way and in His time.

Wives, our prayers and godly behavior will accomplish far more than any words that we could ever speak. In 1 Peter 3:1–2, we are taught to be submissive to our husbands, that even if they don't obey the Word, they, without a word from us, would be won over by our conduct.

Husbands, you must give honor to your wife and treat her with understanding. She may be weaker than you are, but she is your equal partner. Treat her as you should, so your prayers will not be hindered (1 Peter 3:7).

> In the same way, you wives, be submissive to your own husbands [subordinate, not as inferior, but out of respect for the responsibilities entrusted to husbands and their accountability to God, and so partnering with them] so that even if some do not obey the word [of God], they may be won over [to Christ] without discussion by the godly lives of their wives, when they see your modest and respectful behavior [together with your devotion and appreciation—love your husband, encourage him, and enjoy him as a blessing from God]. (1 Peter 3:1–2 AMP)

> In the same way, you husbands, live with your wives in an understanding way [with great gentleness and tact, and

with an intelligent regard for the marriage relationship], as with someone physically weaker, since she is a woman. Show her honor and respect as a fellow heir of the grace of life, so that your prayers will not be hindered or ineffective. (1 Peter 3:7 AMP)

One of the ways that you can put Christ first in your marriage is through daily prayer. Pray for each other and together. There is power when we come into an agreement together through prayer. Another way to put God first in your marriage is to read the Bible or do devotionals together. We have devotional time together with our family every evening before we go to bed. We will watch a Bible story for the little kids, read the Word of God together, then we will always come together and pray. My husband and I will also pray together with just the two of us every morning before we begin our day. It is not about being perfect or having this religious routine; it is about having a heart to love God, obey His commands, and keep Him first in your life.

How do you know if you are putting God's kingdom first? Ask yourself these questions: Do I give Him the first part of my day? Is God the first person I turn to when I need guidance to make decisions? Do I include Him in everything that I do, or do I try to do everything in my own strength? Do I go to the phone or to His throne when circumstances arise? Do I seek God's perspective (His Word and godly counsel), or do I seek the world's perspective? Am I on Facebook, or is my face in His book (the Bible)?

We seek Him first by spending time with Him through prayer, reading His Word, worshipping Him, and being in His presence. We seek Him first when we align ourselves with His truth and walk in His ways. We seek Him first when we abide in Him all throughout the day. It is only when your life is in order that you will experience God's peace, presence, and joy.

So often, women tend to put the kids before their husbands because, let's be honest, kids take a lot of our time and energy. While there are seasons where much of our time goes to raising them, we cannot neglect our spouses. You have to find ways to connect each day, whether that is at night once the kids go to bed or early in the morning. Text or talk throughout the day. My husband and I like to send each other prayers or flirt through our text messages. Take lunch dates each week or have a date night once per month. Find ways to stay connected. I know from my own marriage that it does not take long to disconnect, and before you know it, we will start bickering or misunderstanding one another. We always say that I am not thinking blue and he is not thinking pink when we start acting that way. We know that we need to reconnect and have time together.

One of the best ways for any married couple to connect is through prayer and by being intimate with each other. I know, ladies, some of you do not want to hear that, but it is the truth. God created sex to be enjoyed in a marriage, and it is one of the best ways that you can connect to your spouse. We will talk more about that later because I feel like some of you ladies are going to check out on me right now if I continue talking about that subject. Bear with me, ladies. I can speak from experience that there was a time when I did not enjoy it, but now, with God at the center of our marriage, it gets better and better every single time that my husband and I are intimate. We will get you there slowly but surely … baby steps.

Just like women often put the kids before their husbands, men tend to put their work before their wives. Men have been created to provide and care for their families. They often feel so much pressure to work to make sure that their family is taken care of. Many men also tend to find their identity and purpose in their work. They primarily identify themselves by what they do. If you ever listen to men introduce themselves to one another, they usually ask this question, "What do you do?" They often find their value and worth in what they do rather than in who they are in Christ. They find their purpose in their work and busyness, as do many women.

After Jesus was baptized in the Jordan River by John the Baptist, God the Father spoke from heaven: "This is My beloved Son, in whom I am well pleased" (Matthew 3:17 NKJV). Jesus had not started His ministry yet. He had not healed anyone or performed any miracles, yet His Father said, "I am well pleased with You." God was pleased with who He was and not with what He could do. Jesus's value did not come from His performance. His value came from being the Son of God. The same is true for us. God does not base your value on what you do or how well you perform. Your value is based on the fact that you are His child. God made you in His own image. There is nothing that you can do that will make you more valuable.

No amount of work, title, money, or performance will determine your worth. You can rest knowing that God loves you as His child and there is nothing that you can do to make Him love you any more or any less.

Some men do not understand that their wives just want them to spend some time at home and be present with the family. Husbands, if you are out of balance by working all the time and giving limited time to your wife and family, then it is time to recognize it and make some changes. Sit down and talk to each other to see how you can make changes that would still allow you to bring in the provision for the family but also allow you to spend time together. When my husband was working out of town a lot and getting home late, the situation proved wearisome, not only for him but also for the entire family. We decided that he needed to try to be home by six or six thirty every night so that we could have supper together and spend some time with family. This rule helped us find the balance that we all needed.

Wives, make sure that your home is a place that your husband wants to come home to. If your home is not a place of peace, then that would be a good thing to start working toward. We all know the saying, "If Momma ain't happy, ain't nobody happy." It is true. Women do not realize it, but we truly are the mood setters in our homes. If you want to see why everyone else in the home is not at peace or has an attitude problem, we usually just have to look at ourselves and see that it most often begins with us.

Husbands, this applies to you as well. A negative husband will affect the rest of the family. Just as cancer spreads from cell to cell, so negativity spreads from person to person. Change the atmosphere in your home by changing your attitude. If you want your home to be a place of peace, then you should be at peace.

> Let the peace of Christ [the inner calm of one who walks daily with Him] be the controlling factor in your hearts [deciding and settling questions that arise]. To this peace indeed you were called as members in one body [of believers]. And be thankful [to God always]. (Colossians 3:15 AMP)

> You will keep him in perfect peace, whose mind is stayed on You, because he trusts in You. (Isaiah 26:3 NKJV)

I remember when I first discovered God's peace. It was after I started growing in my relationship with Jesus and would sit with Him, just enjoying His presence and reading the Word of God. You will not experience God's peace apart from Him and His presence. Psalm 100:4 says that we enter into His gates with thanksgiving and into His courts with praise. If you want to enter into God's presence, start by thanking and praising Him. Worship Him with reverence and awe of how great He is. Once you enter into His presence, you will feel the most amazing peace and joy.

Whenever I discovered that I could have peace in my heart every day, I never wanted to go a day without it again. So whenever I am not at peace, I will go sit with the Lord until I am at peace. Our home used to be a place of strife, chaos, and no peace. But once I found Jesus and experienced His peace, I would not allow strife or chaos into our home. People have even said that they feel so much peace when they come into our home.

Proverbs 17:14 (ASV) says, "Starting a quarrel is like opening a floodgate, so stop before a dispute breaks out." We have a rule that when a quarrel starts to break out, we will stop it right away. Sometimes we may even have to walk away from the situation until we can calmly talk about the matter because we know that opening the door to strife will be like opening a floodgate in our home. We are the gatekeepers of our homes. That means we get to allow what comes in and what does not. This means that when the enemy comes to steal, kill, and destroy (John 10:10), we stand against him in prayer. We submit ourselves to God, resist the devil, and he will flee (James 4:7). The enemy is after our marriages, and we must fight for our marriage and family every single day.

If you find yourself not at peace, go back to the place where you lost it. There will be situations and circumstances every day that can cause us to lose our peace, but we have a choice of whether we will allow the enemy to steal our peace and joy. I encourage you to sit with Jesus and ask Him why you lost your peace and why the circumstances caused you to lose it. What is the root? Is it fear? What are you fearing? What is God's truth in the situation? Allow God to speak to your heart. We can still have peace in the midst of any circumstance as long as we have the presence of Jesus. Some people think they can only have peace and joy as long as their circumstances are good. Peace and joy do not come from circumstances but from the presence of God.

Did you know that we can shift the atmosphere in our homes by playing worship music, reading aloud the Word of God, praying, and giving thanks? This is something I do every day so that our home represents a godly atmosphere. A person can also change the atmosphere in their home to a negative one by watching foul movies, listening to ungodly music, speaking profanity, complaining, quarreling, or fighting. You have the power and authority to control the atmosphere in your home. Will it be a place of strife and chaos or a place of love, joy, and peace?

If our marriages are out of alignment, then things will not go well. Everything flows from the top, so if your relationship with the Lord and your spouse is not good, then most likely, nothing else will go well in your life. God must be first, your marriage second, and everything else should come after that. It is amazing how everything flows when we do things God's way. You will never be the husband or wife that you desire to be unless Jesus is Lord of your life, and you have an intimate relationship with Him. To try to live righteously apart from the Righteous One (Jesus), quickening us through the Holy Spirit, is impossible.

If you do not have a relationship with the Lord, or you need to recommit to Him, then do not wait any longer. You and I are not guaranteed tomorrow, and we need to make sure that our salvation is secured. God created us in His own image, and He desires to have an intimate relationship with each one of us. It is not about religion—it's about having a true, intimate relationship with God through His Son, Jesus Christ. "For God so loved the world that He gave His only begotten Son, that whoever believes in Him should not perish but have everlasting life" (John 3:16 NKJV).

God sent His one and only Son, Jesus, to come to earth to live a sinless life and to die on the cross to pay the penalty for our sins and bridge the gap between us and God. The Bible says that Jesus is the Way, the Truth, and the Life and that no one comes to the Father except through Him (John 14:6). You won't get to heaven by just being a good person or doing good deeds. Heaven and hell are real, and there is only one way to get to heaven, and that is through Jesus Christ.

By accepting Him into our hearts through faith by grace, we can be cleansed of our sins and live for eternity in heaven. The Bible says that if we confess our sins, He is faithful and just to forgive us our sins and to cleanse us from all unrighteousness (1 John 1:9). Romans 10:9 (NIV) says, "If you declare with your mouth, 'Jesus is Lord,' and believe in your heart that God raised him from the dead, you will be saved." It is an easy decision and one that you will not regret. If you are ready to make Jesus the Lord over your life, then pray this simple prayer from your heart with me.

Prayer for Salvation

Heavenly Father, I confess that I am a sinner in need of a Savior. I believe that You sent Your Son, Jesus, to come to earth to live a sinless life and to die on the cross for my sins. I believe in my heart that You raised Jesus from the dead. God, forgive me of all my sins and cleanse me of all unrighteousness. I invite You, Jesus, to come into my heart, and I make You Lord over my life in Jesus's name. Amen.

Prayer to Be Filled with the Holy Spirit

The Son of God not only descended from Heaven to save you from your sin, but He also came to baptize you with the Holy Spirit and fire (Matthew 3:11). We need His power to live a life free from the clutches of sin after we have been saved. Because you are a child of God, your Heavenly Father wants to give you the supernatural power that you need to live a new life.

If the Son of God waited for the Holy Spirit to descend upon Him before He began His earthly ministry, how much more do we need the Holy Spirit upon us in order to live our lives? If Jesus needed the baptism of the Holy Spirit, then every believer does. Luke 11:10–13 (NKJV) says, "For everyone who asks receives, and he who seeks finds, and to him who knocks it will be opened. If a son asks for bread from any father among you, will he give him a stone? Or if he asks for a fish, will he give him a serpent instead of a fish? Or if he asks for an egg, will he offer him a scorpion? If you then, being evil, know how to give good gifts to your children, how much more will your heavenly Father give the Holy Spirit to those who ask Him!" All you must do is ask, believe, and receive. Pray to be baptized and filled with the Holy Spirit today.

Heavenly Father, I recognize my need for Your power to live a new life. Fill me with Your Holy Spirit. By faith, I receive it right now. Thank you for baptizing me. Holy Spirit, You are welcome in my life in Jesus's name. Amen.

Summary

- To have a healthy marriage, our lives need to be in alignment.
- When we pursue God's kingdom and His righteousness as our priority for living, then God will take care of everything else in our lives.
- God is a God of order. He wants to be number one in our lives.
- If you want your home to be a place of peace, then you should be at peace.
- Peace and joy do not come from circumstances but from the presence of God.
- God must be first, your marriage second, and everything else should come after that. It is amazing how everything just flows when we do things God's way.
- You will never be the husband or wife that you desire to be unless Jesus is Lord of your life, and you have an intimate relationship with Him. To try to live righteous apart from the Righteous One (Jesus), quickening us through the Holy Spirit, is impossible.

Questions

1. How is the Holy Spirit speaking to me through this chapter?

2. Is God first in my life? Have I submitted my life and my marriage to Him? How can I improve my relationship with Jesus and, therefore, improve my relationship with my spouse?

3. Are my life and my marriage in alignment? Where am I out of alignment? What do I need to do to get into alignment with God and my spouse? What have I put before God and my spouse?

4. Is my home a place of peace? Am I at peace? What changes can I make in my daily routine to spend time with God so I can be at peace?

Prayer

God, help me to be in alignment with You and with my spouse. Do whatever You need to do to get myself and my marriage in order. I want to put you first in my life and in my marriage. I pray that our home will be a place of peace and not of strife. We submit to You, God, and resist the devil so he must flee from our home and marriage in Jesus's name. Amen.

CHAPTER 3

You Are Not His Mother; You Are Not Her Father

Therefore a man shall leave his father and mother and be joined to his wife, and they shall become one flesh.

—Genesis 2:24 (NKJV)

The Bible tells us that we are to leave our father and mother and be joined to our spouse after we marry. It tells us in Genesis 2:24 (KJV), "Therefore shall a man leave his father and his mother, and shall cleave unto his wife: and they shall be one flesh."

This verse does not say that after you leave your mother and father, you have a new mother (your wife) or a new father (your husband). No, it says that now you become one flesh. You are joined together. Your spirits are united. Your spouse is not your child. Women, your husband has a mom; he needs a wife. Men, your wife has a father; she needs a husband.

I am going to speak to the wives first. As women, it is our natural instinct to mother. While this is a wonderful thing as we mother our children, it is not so great when we try to mother our spouse. As moms, we manage a lot of things in the household. We organize the family schedule; take care of the bills; run kids to school and sports activities; do the shopping, cooking, laundry, cleaning; plan birthday parties, help with homework, etc. It seems that there is always a list of things to do. But before long, we can start to treat our spouse as though he is our child and micromanage him. Where we were once a lover and a friend, we have now become a boss and drill sergeant. Your man will not act like a man if you treat him like a child. Instead, lift him up and treat him as the man you married rather than one more person to manage in the household.

Your spouse may begin to resent you for the way that you treat him and, therefore, will not love you the way that you want to be loved. After all, who wants to show love to a woman who just bosses and tries to control everything? Your marriage will go through this continual cycle where the woman who desires to be loved is not getting the love that she wants/needs and the man who desires to be respected is not receiving the respect that he wants/needs. If love and respect are not happening in a marriage, there will be constant tension and strife because both spouses are not receiving what they desire and need most in a marriage. I encourage you to read the book *Love & Respect* by Dr. Emerson Eggerichs.

When husbands are told to love their wives, we can infer that wives need to be loved. When wives are told to respect their husbands, we can infer that husbands need to be respected. Think of it as two kinds of cars that run on different kinds of fuel—diesel and regular. Men run on respect, and women run on love.

Respect is one of the most important things that a man needs to feel from his wife. Men need to feel that they are respected and admired as a person. Sometimes it is difficult to express respect toward your husband when you do not feel that he is acting respectably. There are certain positions that you still give honor and respect to, even if the person is not living up to their potential as a leader. Men are the head of the household, and we are to honor and respect that position of authority.

In 1 Corinthians 11:3, we are told about Christ being the head over every man, and the man is the head of the woman, and God is the head of Christ. Paul is not saying that the husband is superior to the wife. As the Father and Son are equal in essence while different in function, the husband and wife are equal as human beings and in their spiritual standing before God, but different in their roles in marriage. The wife is called to submit to her husband's spiritual leadership but is never to follow her husband into sin or submit to abuse. The man is also called to submit as Christ is the head of every man. He is not free to lead his wife and children however he sees fit; instead, he is to lead in full submission to the Lordship of Christ Jesus.

As husbands and wives, we are to humble ourselves in mutual submission. The husband is not to stand over the wife and dominate her. That is not what Christ did for the church. Jesus Christ laid his life down for the church and He calls husbands to do the same for their wives. When God's people operate within this divine order, there is covering and protection but, like a car, we are in danger of crashing when we get out of alignment.

If you look at the two pictures at the beginning of this chapter, you will see one picture where I am leading my husband along. Then in the next picture, my husband is leading me along. The first picture truly represented what our relationship was like. I was out of order and was doing all the leading and just pulling him along. I was not submitted to my husband and thought that I was the head of the home. I figured that as long as everything went the way that I wanted it to go, then things were good. Oh, how wrong I was! God's Word says that Christ is the head (authority) over every man, man is the head of woman, and God is the head of Christ (1 Corinthians 11:3 AMP). The second picture represents our marriage when we got into our rightful position as husband and wife. I submitted to God and to my husband, which resulted in my husband lovingly leading me and our family. It's a beautiful thing!

But I want you to understand that Christ is the head (authority over) of every man, and man is the head of woman, and God is the head of Christ. (1 Corinthians 11:3 AMP)

For the husband is head of the wife, as also Christ is head of the church; and He is the Savior of the body. (Ephesians 5:23 NKJV)

Women need to feel loved. It is their number one desire, and it is a commandment from God that husbands are to love their wives. God obviously knew that husbands and wives would struggle with love and respect, thus He made it very clear in scripture.

However, each man among you [without exception] is to love his wife as his very own self [with behavior worthy of respect and esteem, always seeking the best for her with an attitude of lovingkindness], and the wife [must see to it] that she respects and delights in her husband [that she notices him and prefers him and treats him with loving concern, treasuring him, honoring him, and holding him dear]. (Ephesians 5:33 AMP)

God instructs us in scripture about how the husband is to treat his wife. Ephesians 5:33 (AMP) says that each man is to love his wife as his very own self (with behavior worthy of respect and esteem, always seeking the best for her with an attitude of lovingkindness) and the wife must see to it that she respects and delights in her husband (that she notices him and prefers him and treats him with loving concern, treasuring him, honoring him, and holding him dear). God also says in 1 Peter 3:7 that a husband is to honor his wife and treat her with understanding. He is to treat her as an heir of Christ so that his prayers will not be hindered.

In the same way, you husbands, live with your wives in an understanding way [with great gentleness and tact, and with an intelligent regard for the marriage relationship], as with someone physically weaker, since she is a woman.

Show her honor and respect as a fellow heir of the grace of
life, so that your prayers will not be hindered or ineffective.
(1 Peter 3:7 AMP)

Husbands, are you loving your wife with behavior that is worthy of
respect and esteem, always seeking the best for her with an attitude of
lovingkindness? Wives, are you respecting and delighting in your husband,
noticing him, preferring him, and treating him with loving concern?

I am aware that there are many relationships where the man is
dominating and controlling and will walk all over his wife as though
she is a doormat. This is not how a marriage should be. Yes, the husband
is the head of the home, but he is to treat his wife as an equal partner,
not lesser than him. We should never have to bow down to or walk on
eggshells around each other. It is never the will of God for any human soul
to be dominated by any other human soul. It is not the will of God for a
husband to dominate his wife, for a wife to dominate her husband, or for
any other person in any situation to dominate and control another person.
The only control that someone else has over you is the control that you
give to them. If you allow a person to control and manipulate you, then it
will continue. If you are currently in an abusive relationship, please seek
help from someone who could give you biblical counseling on what to do
for your situation.

One of the biggest things that I had to learn was that I was not my
husband's mother. I was not created to boss him around and tell him what
to do. I remember getting so irritated when the garage was a mess or when
I would have to tell him that he should get a haircut or help around the
house. My mentor kindly told me that it was not my place to tell him to get
a haircut. If he wanted to look shaggy, then that was on him, but I needed
to come to the place in my heart where I was at peace no matter what, and
I did not let what he did or did not do bother me anymore. I could ask him
to clean the garage or help around the house, but it was not my job to tell
him what to do. Things started to change when I kindly asked him to do
things instead of telling him what to do. I also prayed that he would do
the things that he should, and I was at peace no matter what.

I learned that my husband would respond positively if I just asked him
nicely to do something (in the right tone of voice) rather than complain

or tell him what to do. Sometimes we may be saying the right thing but in the wrong tone of voice. I realized that if I asked in a negative or sharp tone, then my husband would respond in the same way. The Lord worked on me with how I treated and talked to my husband. I felt God ask me one time, "Do you talk to others the way that you talk to your husband when you need something?" To which I replied, "Umm, no." The Lord said, "Then don't talk to him that way." The Lord challenged me to treat my spouse better than the way I treat anyone else. I see so many people who treat their spouse or children worse than anyone else. People will often treat a total stranger better than they do their loved ones. It grieves the Lord's heart when we do this. Our families should get the best of us, not the worst of us. I challenge you just like the Lord challenged me: Treat your spouse and kids better than you would treat anyone else. You definitely will not be able to do it out of your own flesh. But with prayer and the help of the Holy Spirit, He will help you and correct you when you need to be corrected. A simple "Please," "Thank you," and the right tone of voice can go a long way!

> A constant dripping on a day of steady rain and a contentious (quarrelsome) woman are alike; Whoever attempts to restrain her [criticism] might as well try to stop the wind, and grasps oil with his right hand. (Proverbs 27:15–16 AMP)

One thing that keeps me in check is thinking about my sons and how I want their wives to treat them. Is the way that I am acting toward my husband modeling what I want my son to find in a wife? And is the way that I am treating my husband modeling the way that I want my daughters to treat their future husbands? Husbands, is the way that you are treating your wife modeling how you want your daughter to be treated by her future husband or your sons to treat their future wives? Kids will do as they see. How you live your life is their example. Be the example that you want them to be.

Men, God never intended for your role as a husband to be a dominating and controlling father. You are not helping your wife by trying to be her father—you are hindering her. It will create an unhealthy, codependent relationship. Your wife is your helpmate, not a doormat to be walked upon.

When you are devaluing your wife or kids, you are persecuting them, and I believe that you will be judged according to how you treat and raise your family as the head of the household. Husbands are to love their wives as their own bodies for he who loves his wife loves himself (Ephesians 5:28). For no one ever hated his own flesh, but nourishes and cherishes it, just as the Lord does the church (Ephesians 5:29). Husbands, you are to nourish and cherish your wife. You are also not to be harsh with her (Colossians 3:19). If you look at Jesus to be your model, you will find that you are to be a servant-leader to your wife and family. Matthew 20:25–28 says, "But Jesus called them to Himself and said, 'You know that the rulers of the Gentiles lord it over them, and those who are great exercise authority over them. Yet it shall not be so among you; but whoever desires to become great among you, let him be your servant. And whoever desires to be first among you, let him be your slave—just as the Son of Man did not come to be served, but to serve, and to give His life a ransom for many.'"

A spiritual servant-leader imitates Christ. He is tuned in to his family's needs and concerned about their spiritual welfare. He helps them to grow in their relationship with God. He provides support, grace, and encouragement; and he is always ready to protect, help, and defend. A servant-leader would lay down his life for those who have been entrusted to his care.

> So husbands ought to love their own wives as their own bodies; he who loves his wife loves himself. For no one ever hated his own flesh, but nourishes and cherishes it, just as the Lord does the church. (Ephesians 5:28–29 NKJV)

> Husbands, love your wives [with an affectionate, sympathetic, selfless love that always seeks the best for them] and do not be embittered or resentful toward them [because of the responsibilities of marriage]. (Colossians 3:19 AMP)

Men have such an impact on the family when they are leading it in a godly way. Statistics show that if a father is first to find Christ and follow Him, 93 percent of the time the rest of the family will follow. However, if the mother is first to find faith in Christ, 22 percent of the time, the family follows. The men are meant to be the spiritual leaders of the home. Satan knows and understands this. This is why he has been seeking to destroy the family ever since the first family of Adam and Eve. The enemy knows that if he can target the father and keep Him away from God, he can bring him down, ultimately destroying the family.

Men, God has gifted you with an incredible role in your family. I encourage you to step up and be the spiritual servant-leader that God has called you to be.

> The righteous man who walks in integrity and lives life in accord with his [godly] beliefs—How blessed [happy and spiritually secure] are his children after him [who have his example to follow]. (Proverbs 20:7 AMP)

Husbands and wives, take your right position and fulfill the role that God designed for you. If you are a parent, then parent your children, but do not parent your spouse. Treat your spouse and your children the way that you would want to be treated.

> Treat others the same way you want them to treat you. (Luke 6:31 AMP)

Summary

- Your spouse is not your child. Women, your husband has a mom; he needs a wife. Men, your wife has a father; she needs a husband.
- If love and respect are not happening in a marriage, there will be constant tension and strife because both spouses are not receiving what they desire and need most in a marriage.
- Men run on respect, and women run on love.
- As husbands and wives, we are to humble ourselves in mutual submission.
- Sometimes we may be saying the right thing but in the wrong tone of voice.
- Our families should get the best of us, not the worst of us.
- Treat your spouse and children the way that you would want to be treated.

Questions

1. How is the Holy Spirit speaking to me through this chapter?

2. How am I acting toward my spouse? Am I acting like their parent or coming alongside them as their spouse? Is the way that I am treating them honoring the Lord? Am I treating them the way that I would want to be treated?

3. Are we stuck in the continual cycle of not respecting and loving each other? If so, how can we break this cycle and give each other what we both need? Wives, are you respecting your husband the way you should? Take an inventory. How is your tone or attitude toward your husband? Are you being respectful or controlling? Husbands, are you loving your wife the way you should? Take inventory. How is your tone or attitude? Are you being loving or belittling? Do you both agree with how you answered these questions?

4. Husbands, are you leading your wife in a godly way? Are you being a servant-leader? Wives, are you allowing your husband to lead you? Are you honoring and encouraging him to step up and lead your family?

Prayer

Heavenly Father, teach us how to not act like each other's parents but to come alongside each other as a spouse. Help us to respect, love, and honor each other, and by doing so, we will honor You. I pray that You will deal with any controlling spirit that may be operating in either of us. Help us to show love and respect to each other. God, I pray that we would treat each other as we would want to be treated in Jesus's name. Amen.

CHAPTER 4

Your Spouse Is Not Your Source

And my God will liberally supply (fill until full) your every need according to His riches in glory in Christ Jesus.
—Philippians 4:19 (AMP)

God is your source. Everything else is just a resource.

—Tony Evans

It took me a while to figure this one out—that God is my source. Growing up, I learned what most people learn, and that is to work hard, to be independent, and that I am responsible for providing for myself. In high school, I worked two jobs to save up to buy my own car and pay for my own car insurance, gas, and anything else that I wanted. My mom had four kids, and money was tight, so if I wanted anything extra, it was on me to work hard to pay for it. While I believe in hard work and doing what we need to do to provide for ourselves and our families, I had to change my (performance) mindset that it was not all on me and that I didn't have to strive to make it happen. I had to learn to trust God and that He would provide for everything that I needed with the resources that He brought to my life.

My husband and I are entrepreneurs, and we both left our fixed-income jobs to start our own businesses within six months of each other. We followed God's lead and took the leap of faith. It was scary at first, but God always provided if we kept Him first and gave Him the first tenth (tithe) of our income. We learned that tithing was not just something that churches preached but was a biblical principle that God requires of His people to show that He is first in our finances and lives. The command to tithe is a command to recognize God's ownership of everything in our lives. You may think that your job, bank account, or spouse is your source, but they are just a resource. God is responsible for the money and resources that we have, but He wants to make sure that we recognize that He is our source. Everything that we have is the Lord's. All He is asking is that we give the *first* 10 percent of our income back to Him.

Do Not Rob God

"Will a man rob God? Yet you have robbed Me! But you say, 'In what way have we robbed You?' In tithes and offerings. You are cursed with a curse, for you have robbed Me, even this whole nation. Bring all the tithes into the storehouse, that there may be food in My house, and try

Me now in this," says the LORD of hosts, "If I will not open for you the windows of heaven and pour out for you such blessing that there will not be room enough to receive it. And I will rebuke the devourer for your sakes, so that he will not destroy the fruit of your ground, nor shall the vine fail to bear fruit for you in the field," says the LORD of hosts; "and all nations will call you blessed, for you will be a delightful land," says the LORD of hosts. (Malachi 3:10–12 NKJV)

As entrepreneurs with no fixed income, we have witnessed God come through for our family time and time again as we put God first in our finances. But we have also experienced drought like we had never seen before when we were not giving God the first and best part of our income. We went through a season of hardship (one thing after the next), and it was hard to pay the bills. Out of fear, we began to pay the bills first and give God whatever was left. Let me tell you, that did not work for us at all. We went through a season where it was as though everything was being robbed from us. We had car problems, appliance breakdowns, medical and dental bills, etc. I was on maternity leave with our fifth child, and suddenly, my husband had no work coming in. We were up to our necks in bills, and things just kept piling up. It was devastating and humiliating. I remember not even having food in the refrigerator, and our kids would open it to look for something to eat. I would just go to my room and cry, praying to God for help.

Somehow, some money would always come in, so we always had enough food for that day, but we were still struggling to pay the bills. We were crying out to God, asking Him to show us what we were doing wrong and what we needed to do. It was then that the Lord convicted us that we were not giving Him our first fruits and were actually putting Him last by giving Him our leftovers.

You may think you do not have money to tithe, but I am telling you right now that you can't afford *not* to tithe. We learned our lesson. As soon as we repented to God for not giving Him the first 10 percent of our income and started tithing like we should, giving Him the very *first* of our income, things turned around for us. We learned our lesson with tithing and want to honor the Lord with the best of every part of our lives.

> Honor the LORD with your possessions, and with the firstfruits of all your increase. (Proverbs 3:9 NKJV)

I remember another time when money was tight, and I started harping on my husband, saying that he needed to provide for us. Immediately, I heard the Lord say to me so clearly, "Do not speak to your husband like that again. He is not your source. I am your source." It stopped me in my tracks. I have never heard the Lord speak that loud to me before, and I will not forget it. God corrected me out of His great love. He humbled me and changed me. From that day forward, I looked to the Lord as my source, my provider, my Jehovah Jireh. Genesis 22:14 is the first time in scripture where God is called Jehovah Jireh (the Lord will provide). It was during a moment when Abraham was being obedient to God to offer up his son, Isaac as a sacrifice. God provided a ram in the thicket in place of the sacrifice of Abraham's son. Abraham called that place Jehovah-Jireh: as it is said to this day, in the mount of the Lord, it shall be seen (Genesis 22:14 KJV).

Ladies, our husbands are not our God. Anytime that we put our spouse in a place to be our God, we will be disappointed and frustrated because they will never be able to fulfill a role that only God can fill in our lives. We often expect our husbands to provide for us emotionally and spiritually, and we forget to cling to the Lord. Yes, we are to fulfill the roles in marriage that God has given us (see Ephesians 5:21–33), but we are never to be codependent on each other and believe that our spouse will meet all our needs because they just won't. There is a God-shaped hole in every one of our hearts that only God Himself, our Creator, can fulfill. No amount of money, possessions, status, work, accomplishments, friends, social media followers, etc., will ever be able to fill that void in our hearts. If you have found yourself relying on your spouse or anything else in this world to bring you fulfillment, then repent and turn your heart back to the Lord—back to your first love.

I have witnessed many marriages fail because one of the spouses was searching for fulfillment in all the wrong places. If you are not spending time with Jesus every day and filling yourself with His Holy Word, you will try to find fulfillment in food, shopping, social media, addictions, money, lust, possessions, titles, hobbies, relationships, etc. The sad truth is none of that will ever be enough to satisfy you. It will always leave you feeling empty and searching for the next "thing." Many marriages have failed because one or both spouses were searching for satisfaction in all the wrong places. A new partner is only going to bring you temporary happiness. Give it time, and that same emptiness and dissatisfaction will remain in your heart until you fill it with the only One who can satisfy, and that is Christ Jesus.

> No love of the natural heart is safe unless the human heart
> has been satisfied by God *first*.
>
> —Oswald Chambers

King Solomon had everything he could ever want in life. He had money, possessions, fame, power, wisdom, seven hundred wives, and three hundred concubines. I still do not understand how the wisest man in the world thought that it was wise to have one thousand women in his life. That is just asking for trouble! But he thought it would fulfill him, and he later discovered that after all his experiences, Solomon declared that everything was meaningless and purposeless. It was like chasing after the wind. Materially, we can never have enough. There will always be an appetite for more, and it will never fulfill us.

> I have seen all the works which have been done under the
> sun, and behold, all is vanity, a futile grasping and chasing
> after the wind. (Ecclesiastes 1:14 AMP)

If we are not looking to God to meet our daily physical, mental, emotional, and spiritual needs, then we will always come up empty and discouraged. I found that anytime I started placing people and things before the Lord, He would begin to remove them because they had become an idol to me. God will remove the props that you have leaned against (finances, relationships, jobs, bank accounts, friends, mentors, etc.) to get you to rely upon Him. I remember a season in my life when God stripped everything away from me until all I had was the Lord and my family. It was a very painful season as I could not understand what was happening at the time until the Lord taught me that I was putting my identity and security in all those things, and they needed to be in Him. Sometimes depending on God requires losing everything else we have depended on. Then we can focus on what is important—having the right relationship with God. More than anything else in this world, we need God. Are you relying on something other than God in your life?

> You never know God is all you need until God is all you have.
> —Rick Warren

Our identity is in Christ. We are not defined by what we do or what we have done in the past. We are not our sins, failures, or what others think or say about us. Our identity comes from God and who He says we are. To be able to understand your identity as a follower of Christ, you need to understand how He sees you. Your identity is ultimately based on what God has done for you. In the Bible, God tells us about how He views His people (for those who have received Jesus as their Lord and Savior).

In Christ, you are loved (Jeremiah 31:3, Romans 5:8, John 3:16, Galatians 2:20, John 15:13, Ephesians 3:16–18). You were created with a purpose (Ephesians 2:10). You are not just a carbon copy of someone else. You were created in the image of the Almighty God (Genesis 1:27). When God made you, He threw away the mold. There is only one of you, and you are His masterpiece (Ephesians 2:10). You are fearfully and wonderfully made (Psalm 139:14).

In Christ, you are not only loved, you are chosen (John 15:16, 1 Peter 2:9). God sent His own Son to earth to die in your place so that you could be included in His family, as a child of God (John 1:12). You are not a mistake. Even if others have rejected or abandoned you, you are chosen and wanted by God. He loves you no matter what.

In Christ, you are forgiven (Ephesians 4:32, Colossians 3:13, Psalm 103:10–14, 1 John 1:9). Because Jesus, who was without sin, died the death you should have on the cross, you can be forgiven of sin. This forgiveness allows you to be considered a child of God. Therefore, in God's eyes, if you have accepted what Jesus did for you, you are completely forgiven. Your sins have been removed as far as the east is from the west (Psalm 103:12).

In Christ, you are redeemed (Ephesians 1:7, Colossians 1:13–14). Christ's sacrifice has bought you back from the forces of sin and evil that once owned and controlled you and made you His. When God looks at you, He does not see a former sinner. He does not see you in light of who you once were. He sees you as redeemed: a new creation (2 Corinthians 5:17) who has been made whole. You do not have to define yourself by your past mistakes. God does not do that. You can walk in the identity of someone who is made new in Christ. You have been redeemed by the precious blood of Jesus.

In Christ, you are adopted (Ephesians 1:5). You have been adopted into God's family. You are considered a child of God, having all the rights and standing of Jesus, His Son. Just as earthly adoption is a legally binding process that names you a permanent part of a family, heavenly adoption is just as permanent and binding. You are His child, and He will never take that away.

If you put your faith in Jesus, you have a new identity in Him. The more you get to know Jesus through His Word and time in prayer, the more you will understand your identity in Him. Let the One who created you be the One who defines you.

God is our source. He is the only one who can save us, redeem us, define us, heal us, and provide for our every need. May we always look to Him as our One True Source and trust that He will bring the resources.

> And God is able to make all grace [every favor and earthly blessing] come in abundance to you, so that you may always [under all circumstances, regardless of the need] have complete sufficiency in everything [being completely self-sufficient in Him], and have an abundance for every good work and act of charity. (2 Corinthians 9:8 AMP)

Summary

- God is your source. Everything else is just a resource.
- You may think that you do not have money to tithe, but I am telling you right now that you can't afford *not* to tithe.
- Anytime we put our spouse in a place to be our God, we will be disappointed and frustrated because they will never be able to fulfill a role that only God can fill in our lives.

- There is a God-shaped hole in every one of our hearts that only God Himself, our Creator, can fulfill.
- If we are not looking to God to meet our daily physical, mental, emotional, and spiritual needs, then we will always come up empty and discouraged.
- Our identity comes from God and who He says we are.
- God is our source. He is the only one who can save us, redeem us, define us, heal us, and provide for our every need.

Questions

1. How is the Holy Spirit speaking to me through this chapter?

2. Do I believe that God is my source? Have I looked to my spouse to be my source instead of looking to God?

3. What have I been seeking to fulfill me? What would it look like to go to God instead of another person or thing for fulfillment?

4. Which verse about who you are in Christ (your identity) spoke to you the most?

Prayer

God, I repent for putting anyone or anything before You. You are my source, and I look to You to provide for my every need. Forgive me for the times that I have looked to my spouse as my source instead of looking to You. Help me to come to know my identity that is found in You in Jesus's mighty name. Amen.

CHAPTER 5

Marriage Is Not Fifty-Fifty

Do nothing from selfishness or empty conceit [through factional motives, or strife], but with [an attitude of] humility [being neither arrogant nor self-righteous], regard others as more important than yourselves. Do not merely look out for your own personal interests, but also for the interests of others.

—Philippians 2:3–4 (AMP)

You have probably heard the saying that marriage is fifty-fifty. I disagree. While we all most likely go into marriage with a fifty-fifty plan, the reality is it doesn't work that way. Marriage is often lopsided, where one spouse will put in more effort than the other. But eventually, it can flip in the other direction. We all go through seasons of life, with highs and lows, mountaintops and valleys. Your spouse may be going through a valley while you are sitting on a mountaintop. I personally have found that when I am struggling and feeling weak, my husband is strong and is there to encourage me, and vice versa. We are there to hold each other up.

> Two are better than one, because they have a good reward for their labor. For if they fall, one will lift up his companion. But woe to him who is alone when he falls, for he has no one to help him up. Again, if two lie down together, they will keep warm; but how can one be warm alone? Though one may be overpowered by another, two can withstand him. And a threefold cord is not quickly broken. (Ecclesiastes 4:9–12 NKJV)

A marriage will never be perfect, where each spouse is giving fifty-fifty. With our selfish human nature, we often look out for our own interests and are consumed with our personal schedules, conflicts, and thoughts. It takes dying to our selfish nature daily to consider others more than ourselves and to look out for the interests of others. In a marriage, there will be different seasons of life where one spouse just cannot possibly give as much as they would want to give. Whether it be working long hours, going through a health issue, taking care of small children, being a caretaker of a parent, experiencing a loss, etc., the other spouse will carry the load for that time or season.

A fifty-fifty relationship implies that you are keeping the score of every deed you do. We cannot expect our spouses to reciprocate everything that we do for them. Marriage is not a competition about who is putting in more effort, or "If you will do this, then I will do that." That is a selfish attitude, and God will never bless selfishness. What God will bless is when we honor and serve our spouse out of humility and love, regarding our spouse as more important than ourselves. "God opposes the proud, but He gives grace to the humble" (James 4:6 NLT).

My husband used to do so many little things for me such as starting the coffee, writing on my mirror, complimenting me, filling my car with gas, etc.; and I was so busy with work and kids that I didn't always take the time to do it back. But now I've learned to take the time to do the little things in order to serve him. We should continually ask ourselves this question, "How can I better serve my spouse?"

A Christian marriage should be based on selfless, biblical love. The agape love that 1 Corinthians 13 describes is the highest form of love—a selfless, sacrificial, unconditional kind of love. It has nothing to do with reciprocation or effort on the part of the other. It is loving someone regardless of what they are doing. A Christian's wedding vow to love until death is not a conditional contract; rather, it is an unconditional covenant before God that does not depend on the other's effort.

The Excellence of Love

If I speak with the tongues of men and of angels, but have not love [for others growing out of God's love for me], then I have become only a noisy gong or a clanging cymbal [just an annoying distraction]. And if I have the gift of prophecy [and speak a new message from God to the people], and understand all mysteries, and [possess] all knowledge; and if I have all [sufficient] faith so that I can remove mountains, but do not have love [reaching out to others], I am nothing. If I give all my possessions to feed the poor, and if I surrender my body to be burned, but do not have love, it does me no good at all. Love endures with patience and serenity, love is kind and thoughtful, and is not jealous or envious; love does not brag and is not proud or arrogant. It is not rude; it is not self-seeking; it is not provoked [nor overly sensitive and easily angered]; it does not take into account a wrong endured. It does not rejoice at injustice, but rejoices with the truth [when right and truth prevail]. Love bears all things [regardless of what comes], believes all things [looking for the best in each one], hopes all things [remaining steadfast during difficult times], endures all things [without weakening]. (1 Corinthians 13:1–7 AMP) Love never fails (it never fades nor ends). (1 Corinthians 13:1-8 AMP)

A contract marriage is an "I will if you ..." exchange. You and your spouse have an unspoken arrangement, in which each of you is committed to meeting each other's needs, as long as they are meeting yours. Unfortunately, our world promotes this view of marriage. Marriage is often portrayed as an arrangement primarily geared to our happiness and fulfillment. If our needs are met, marriage is valued. But when our spouse is no longer meeting our needs, we are led to believe that it is okay to withdraw or to walk away. No one fulfills the needs of a spouse perfectly. For that reason, an "I will, if you ..." marriage is ultimately a recipe for tension and discord.

When you approach marriage as a covenant, you are entering into a partnership that is an "I will, because ..." foundation. In a marriage covenant, you are committing yourself to loving, serving, and meeting the needs of your spouse simply because you love them and because you made a vow to them and to God. The marriage covenant was intended to reflect the love and relationship between Christ and His church. When the apostle Paul talks about marriage in Ephesians 5, he reminds us that Christian marriages are patterned after Christ's love for the church. We are to love our spouse in the same manner that Jesus loves his church. God's relationship with His people is defined by covenant—not contract. He is faithful to us even when we are faithless and loves us far beyond what we deserve.

God does not just love us or meet our needs as a response to what we do for Him, He cares for us and loves us because He created us, and it is who He is (1 John 4:8). He loved us so much that He sent His one and only Son, Jesus, to die on the cross to pay the penalty for our sins so that whoever believes in Him will have eternal life (John 3:16). When we grasp God's covenant love for us and receive it, only then can we extend it to others. You cannot give away something that you do not have. So to love others, you must first love God and receive the great love that He has for you. It does not matter what you have done in the past ... God loves you.

There is nothing that you can do for God to love you anymore or any less. He loves you. Period. Receive it, and then give it away.

> Beloved, let us [unselfishly] love and seek the best for one another, for love is from God; and everyone who loves [others] is born of God and knows God [through personal experience]. The one who does not love has not become acquainted with God [does not and never did know Him], for God is love. [He is the originator of love, and it is an enduring attribute of His nature]. (1 John 4:7–8 AMP)
>
> The absence or presence of love for others indicates the absence or presence of love for God.
>
> —Tony Evans

You may be thinking, *Well, I don't feel love towards my spouse.* Or maybe you have fallen out of love. Well, you can fall back in love because love is a choice. You will not always *feel* like loving your spouse, but you can *choose* to. I remember a time early in our marriage when I did not feel love toward my husband. The butterflies had gone away, and it seemed that all we did was fight. It is hard to feel love toward a person when you are constantly angry with them. I remember that year, we attended several weddings, and 1 Corinthians 13 was recited at every single wedding. I know that 1 Corinthians 13:4–8 are popular wedding verses, but I could feel that God was speaking to me every time these scriptures were read. He was pricking my heart and showing me that real love is not butterflies or goosebumps. Real love is true biblical love listed in those verses.

I had to start praying for God to help me love my husband the way that he wanted me to love him because I could not do it out of my own flesh. I also found that the more I fell in love with Jesus and the closer I became to God in my faith walk, the more I loved my husband and the closer I became to him. The more that we both grew in our relationship with Christ, the closer we became to each other. You have probably seen the illustration of the triangle with God at the top and the man/woman in the bottom corners. The idea is that the closer the man and the woman get to God, the closer they become to each other. It is definitely true!

I have been a personal trainer for twenty-two years now, and I always tell my clients that they will get out exactly what they put in. If you put a level 10-effort in, you will get a 10 out. If you give a 3-effort, do not expect to get the results that come from a level 10 work ethic. It just does not work that way. The same goes for your marriage. Whatever you put into your marriage is what you are going to get out of it. If you put only a little effort into your marriage, you are not going to get much out of it. The more you put into something, the better it becomes and the greater the results. What are you willing to put into your marriage?

Marriage is a commitment, and it takes work. It is not easy, but it is one of the greatest blessings and gifts from God to share life with someone else. If your marriage is not what you want it to be, then do what you need to do to improve it. It will not get better if you don't do anything at all. It is like getting healthy and losing weight. Nothing happens unless you start making changes, and small changes add up over time to make big changes.

If you start to cut out soda or sugary drinks and replace them with water, you will begin to see some results. Then if you remove all the fried and processed foods, you will see more results. You start exercising, and you begin to feel and look better. People begin to notice changes. Then you take it a step further and begin eating more lean protein, complex carbs, healthy fats, fruits, and vegetables. You are mindful of what's going into your body. You wake up one day and you are down twenty or thirty pounds and have more energy than you ever had. It is all because of the little changes that added up over time. It is the same with marriages. All the little things will add up to yield big results.

> If the grass looks greener on the other side, it's time to water your own yard.
>
> —Unknown

I have always loved the quote, "If the grass looks greener on the other side, it's time to water your own yard." It is easy to look at other marriages and think that they somehow have it all together, or that another couple's marriage is perfect, but there is no such thing as a perfect marriage. It is also easy when our marriage is not good to start looking around and think that we would be better off with someone else. That is a lie straight from the pit of hell. The enemy wants nothing more than to destroy your marriage and family. If you ever start looking, comparing, or thinking that the grass is greener somewhere else, it is time to water your own yard.

How do you take care of your lawn? You plant seed, water, watch the seed grow, pull the weeds, water some more, mow the grass, weed eat, water again, fertilize, pull some more weeds, and keep on watering. In your marriage, you plant a seed by doing all the little things you did when you first dated each other: you gave each other attention, complimented each other, wrote notes, called, texted (if you had phones back then), actually talked (that's a big one for some of you), and simply spent time together.

You water the seed with love and kindness. You start to watch the seeds grow by continuing to love your spouse the way you did before you were married. You pull any unhealthy weeds that are hurting your marriage— the negative words, unforgiveness, bitterness, lust, pride, selfishness, etc. You mow your lawn by putting in the effort to spend time together, to have conversations, and to work on your marriage. You weed eat or trim the extra weeds by nipping the little things before they become bigger things. There is a scripture in Song of Solomon 2:15 (AMP) that says, "Catch the foxes for us, the little foxes that spoil and ruin the vineyards (of love), while our vineyards are in blossom." The "little foxes" in this context refer to those sins, attitudes, and habits that we more often overlook, excuse, or defend. Deal with the "little foxes" before they spoil your marriage.

We then fertilize our yards by putting each other first, spending time together in prayer, being intimate, and doing whatever we need to do to make sure our grass is green. You can tell who takes care of their lawns just by looking. When you see a lawn that is luscious green, trimmed, and has no weeds, you know that the owners have put a lot of time and effort into their yard. On the contrary, when you see a yard that is overgrown, full of weeds, and turning brown, you know that the owners have not put in the time that the yard requires.

I believe that others can see if our marriage is truly good or not. You can tell what is fake and what is genuine. When you see a marriage that you would admire, you know that they have put the time and effort into it. It did not just come easy. So the next time you see a healthy biblical marriage that you would want yours to look like, start doing the things that you know you need to do and watch yours begin to flourish. It may not be easy, but it will always be worth it!

Remember, you will get out of your marriage whatever effort that you put into it. Don't expect to have level 10 results if you've only been willing to put in a level 5 effort. Your marriage is worth your time and effort. What are you willing to put into it?

Summary

- Marriage is not a competition about who is putting in more effort or "If you will do this, then I will do that."
- A Christian marriage should be based on selfless, biblical love.
- In a marriage covenant, you are committing yourself to loving, serving, and meeting the needs of your spouse simply because you love them and because you made a vow to them and to God.
- When we grasp God's covenant love for us and receive it, only then can we extend it to others.
- You will not always *feel* like loving your spouse, but you can *choose* to.
- "If the grass looks greener on the other side, it's time to water your own yard."
- "Little foxes" refers to those sins, attitudes, and habits that we more often overlook, excuse, or defend. Deal with the "little foxes" before they spoil your marriage.

Questions

1. How is the Holy Spirit speaking to me through this chapter?

2. How have I viewed my marriage (contract or covenant)? Do I expect my spouse to do whatever I do for them, or do I give without expecting anything in return?

3. What level of effort have I been putting into my marriage? What can I do to increase my effort level?

4. What can I do to tend to my own "lawn" to make it healthier and greener? What seeds can I sow? What weeds need to be pulled? How can I water it?

Prayer

Lord, help me tend to my marriage. Show me what seeds I can sow, what weeds need to be pulled, and how I can water my marriage. Give me the strength, patience, and endurance to continue sowing as I watch it grow and flourish in Jesus's name. Amen.

CHAPTER 6

See the Way That God Sees

But the LORD said to Samuel, "Do not look at his appearance or at his physical stature, because I have refused him. For the LORD does not see as man sees; for man looks at the outward appearance, but the LORD looks at the heart.

—1 Samuel 16:7 (NKJV)

I remember a time in our marriage when it was hard. We were at odds, irritated with each other, and I did not even want to look at my husband. I knew that my heart was not right, so I began to pray that God would help me to see my husband the way that He sees him. I also prayed that God would help me love him the way that I used to love him when we first started dating. I kept praying those prayers over and over. I will never forget the day that I showed up to my daughter's dance class since it was Parents' Day, and we were allowed to come watch. I remember sitting there watching her, and I saw my husband walking up through the windows. As I watched him walk up and open the door to come in, I literally got butterflies in my stomach, as though it was my first time seeing him again. I felt this overwhelming love in my heart for him, and I believe that God had answered my prayers. It was something that I could have never mustered up on my own. God helped me to see him again through His eyes of love.

We need God's eyes to love. If not, we will only love when we "feel" love or love those that are easy to love. If we love only those that are easy to love, what credit is that to us? Even sinners love those who love them. Love is not a feeling; it is a choice.

> If you [only] love those who love you, what credit is that to you? For even sinners love those who love them. If you do good to those who do good to you, what credit is that to you? For even sinners do the same. If you lend [money] to those from whom you expect to receive [it back], what credit is that to you? Even sinners lend to sinners expecting to receive back the same amount. But love [that is, unselfishly seek the best or higher good for] your enemies, and do good, and lend, expecting nothing in return; for your reward will be great (rich, abundant), and you will be sons of the Most High; because He Himself is kind and gracious and good to the ungrateful and the wicked. Be merciful (responsive, compassionate, tender) just as your [heavenly] Father is merciful. (Luke 6:32–36 AMP)

What about loving someone who has deeply hurt you or loving someone in sin? How does God view that person? Does He reject them? He did not even reject those who were nailing Him to a tree. Jesus said in Luke 23:34 (NKJV), "Father forgive them; for they do not know what they do." Jesus forgave those who beat, spat, scourged, and mocked Him while He was hanging on the cross. For many of us, it takes months and years for us to finally forgive a person who hurt us. But if we look at the life of Jesus, we will see that He forgave while the wounds were still fresh. When I discovered that revelation, I was walking through a time of hurt by someone close, and I chose to apply that to my situation. As hard as it was to utter those words, I said, "Father forgive them for they do not know what they do."

As the hurt persisted for years, I would have to repeat praying that verse and remind myself that love keeps no records of wrongs (1 Corinthians 13:5). Our flesh wants to hold on to everything that has ever been done to us. But that is a miserable way to live. Unforgiveness will only keep us stuck and locked in our own prisons. Having unforgiveness toward somebody is not hurting them; it is hurting ourselves. Satan uses that as an inroad into our lives. It will stop the blessing of God. When we do not forgive, we ourselves will not be forgiven (Matthew 6:15).

You may say, "Well, you don't know what they did to me?" No, I do not. But I know what was done to Jesus, and yet He still forgave. He took all our sins upon His shoulders in order that we may be forgiven. What a price that He paid! We did not deserve to have our sins forgiven, but He chose to forgive us anyway by dying on the cross and paying the penalty for all our past and future sins. All of us sin and fall short of the glory of God (Romans 3:23). We live in a fallen world, and unfortunately, there is sin that hurts people. Hurt people hurt other people, but healed people heal other people. You must get healed from the hurts of the past, and that happens through a process called forgiveness.

> If you don't heal from what hurt you, you will bleed on people who didn't cut you.
>
> —Unknown

Offense, unforgiveness, and bitterness spread. They do not just affect you, they also affect the people around you. It is like a virus that spreads and infects others.

> Pursue peace with all people, and holiness, without which no one will see the Lord: looking carefully lest anyone fall short of the grace of God; lest any root of bitterness springing up cause trouble, and by this many become defiled. (Hebrews 12:14–15 NKJV)

> Let all bitterness and wrath and anger and clamor [perpetual animosity, resentment, strife, fault-finding] and slander be put away from you, along with every kind of malice [all spitefulness, verbal abuse, malevolence]. Be kind and helpful to one another, tender-hearted [compassionate, understanding], forgiving one another [readily and freely], just as God in Christ also forgave you. (Ephesians 4:31–32 AMP)

How do you forgive? You choose to. You ask the Lord for help. You pray. You meditate on what God's Word says about forgiveness. Most of the time, it is not a one-time prayer; instead, it is a process of praying each day and allowing God to work in your heart. You cannot stay mad at a person if you pray for them and bless them every day. God will eventually change your heart. It may start out with a prayer of you dreadfully uttering the words under your breath to forgive them. But as you continue to pray for them, asking God to help you see them through His eyes, He will eventually change your heart and give you compassion for the person. Forgiveness does not mean that the relationship will be restored, although it can be. Sometimes, to protect yourself from continuing to get hurt, you may have to sever that relationship, but you can still forgive. But what if they keep on hurting you? You forgive again.

> Then Peter came to Him and asked, "Lord, how many times will my brother sin against me and I forgive him and let it go? Up to seven times?" Jesus answered him, "I say to you, not up to seven times, but seventy times seven." (Matthew 18:21–22 AMP)

Life is not fair because there is sin in the world. But God has seen every hurt in your life, and one day, He will make all the wrongs right. God is our vindicator. When we give our hurts to Him and forgive as He commands us to do, He makes the wrongs right. He does a way better job of vindicating us than we could ever do for ourselves. Our God is a loving God, but He is also a God of justice. To allow evil to hurt his children and not seek justice would be unloving. God is very aware of what people have done to you, and there will be a day of reckoning. Trust Him to right your wrongs as you choose to forgive.

> For the LORD will judge His people, and He will have compassion on His servants. (Psalm 135:14 NKJV)

> Beloved, never avenge yourselves, but leave the way open for God's wrath [and His judicial righteousness]; for it is written [in Scripture], "Vengeance is mine, I will repay," says the LORD. (Romans 12:19 AMP)

When we see through a different perspective with God's eyes rather than through our flesh, it will make all the difference. I remember watching a woman one time be so harsh with her little three-year-old daughter. It broke my heart, and as I was watching her, I found myself passing judgment upon her at first. Then I stopped judging and prayed for her. I asked God to help me see her through His eyes and what was really going on. Suddenly, I saw a visual in my mind of a heart that had holes all through it (as though it had been pierced with a pitchfork), and blood was gushing from those holes. I saw how hurt her heart was and that she was unknowingly taking it out on her daughter. I felt that I was supposed to pray for her and tell her that she was a good mom. I also felt led to pray for the healing of her wounded heart. We were both in tears as I prayed for her. As I told her that she was a good mom, she just sobbed. God knew that was what she needed to hear. If I had just judged her without praying and asking God to see her through His eyes, I never would have had that revelation and would not have been able to pray effectively for her. Only God knows what is truly going on in each person's heart. The next time that you are tempted to judge a person, why don't you stop and ask God what is going on in their heart and to help you see with His eyes of compassion?

> Do not judge and criticize and condemn [others unfairly with an attitude of self-righteous superiority as though assuming the office of a judge], so that you will not be judged [unfairly]. For just as you [hypocritically] judge others [when you are sinful and unrepentant], so will you be judged; and in accordance with your standard of measure [used to pass out judgment], judgment will be measured to you. Why do you look at the [insignificant] speck that is in your brother's eye, but do not notice and acknowledge the [egregious] log that is in your own eye? Or how can you say to your brother, 'Let me get the speck out of your eye,' when there is a log in your own eye? You hypocrite (play-actor, pretender), first get the log out of your own eye, and then you will see clearly to take the speck out of your brother's eye. (Matthew 7:1–5 AMP)

Before Jesus ever healed anyone, He would have compassion on them. If we are to be a witness and help other people, we need to be filled with His compassion. If you are struggling to love and have compassion for your spouse, then start praying for God to give it to you.

I can honestly say that I love my husband so much more now than I did on the day that we said, "I do." I am still attracted to him and will tell him many times just how "hot" he is. After twenty-three years of marriage, I am so thankful that we still find each other attractive and love one another.

Wives, you need to take notice of your husband and affirm him. Your husband needs your attention and words of affirmation. I remember one time when I was busy cooking supper, and my husband tried to show me some of his work that he had just done. He was trying to show me a picture on his phone, and I just barely glanced at it and said, "Uh-huh" and then went on to what I was doing. The next day, I met with my spiritual mentor, and she just so happened to ask me how my husband was doing and whether I was giving him the attention that he needed. I was so convicted and shared what had happened the day before. She said something to me that I will never forget.

She said, "If you won't give him the attention that he needs, then someone else will." Wow! I don't want to be the reason that my husband seeks attention or affirmation from another source. I want to do my part as his wife to notice him, affirm him, and make sure he knows that he is seen and valued.

Husbands, when was the last time that you affirmed your wife? Your wife needs to hear you affirm her daily. She needs to hear that you think she is beautiful and that you love her. You may say, "Well, she knows that I love her, so I don't need to say it all the time." That is wrong. Your wife needs to hear you tell her often that you love her. Women are emotional beings and need to feel loved. Husbands, affirm your wife, so she will not be looking for that attention elsewhere.

One time, I did a weight loss and exercise challenge for some ladies. Each day, I would have a devotional for them to read and a daily challenge. One specific day, I talked about thankfulness, and I encouraged them to write a note to someone that they were thankful for. One woman told me that she wrote an encouraging note to her husband. When her husband read it, he started crying, asking her what was wrong, and if she was dying. It is funny, but it's not. Her husband obviously had not heard those words for a long time and needed to hear them. Why don't we tell our loved ones more often how we feel about them? Do not wait until your loved ones pass away before you express your feelings toward them. You may not get the chance tomorrow. Appreciate your spouse and the people in your life and love them like there is no tomorrow.

> LORD, let me know my [life's] end, and [to appreciate] the extent of my days; Let me know how frail I am [how transient is my stay here]. (Psalm 39:4 AMP)

> So teach us to number our days, that we may gain a heart of wisdom. (Matthew 7:1–5 AMP)

If you are not seeing or treating your spouse the way that you should, pray and ask God to give you His eyes to see them. Take your frustrations to the Lord and allow Him to give you a new perspective. Allow God to soften your heart so that you can love your spouse the way that He wants you to love them. Just as God has loved us, so He wants us to love one another (John 13:34).

> I am giving you a new commandment, that you love one another. Just as I have loved you, so you too are to love one another. By this everyone will know that you are My disciples if you have love and unselfish concern for one another. (John 13:34–35 AMP)

Summary

- We need God's eyes to love.
- Love is not a feeling; it is a choice.
- "If you don't heal from what hurt you, you will bleed on people who didn't cut you." - Unknown
- When we see through a different perspective with God's eyes, rather than through our flesh, it will make all the difference.
- If you are struggling to love and have compassion for your spouse, then start praying for God to give it to you.
- Wives, you need to take notice of your husband and affirm him. Your husband needs your attention and words of affirmation.
- Husbands, your wife needs to hear you tell her often that you love her. Women are emotional beings and need to feel loved.

Questions

1. How is the Holy Spirit speaking to me through this chapter?

2. Do I need to forgive my spouse for anything? What hurt do I need to give to Jesus to help heal my heart?

3. Am I seeing my spouse through God's eyes or through my flesh? Am I choosing to love even when I do not "feel" like it? If not, pray and ask God to help you see them through His eyes and to love them the way that He does.

4. Am I taking notice of my spouse and affirming them? In what ways can I encourage them more?

Prayer

Lord, please give me Your eyes to see others how You see them. Help me to have compassion and love others the way You do. Show me the way that You see my spouse and fill my heart with the same love that You have for them. Help me to forgive my spouse or anyone who has hurt me and mend any brokenness in my heart in Jesus's name. Amen.

CHAPTER 7

Safeguard Your Marriage

Therefore what God has joined together, let not man separate.
—Mark 10:9 (NKJV)

According to the dictionary, the definition of the word *safeguard* is "a measure taken to protect someone or something," or "to prevent something undesirable." I believe that one of the reasons that some marriages fail is they do not safeguard their marriage. We must have guardrails up to protect our marriage and prevent something undesirable from happening. Nobody goes into a marriage and hopes for a divorce, plans for an affair, or wants to fight. It is the enemy who comes to steal, kill, and destroy (John 10:10). If we do not safeguard our marriage by keeping the doors closed to the enemy, then he will come to destroy it. It is not a matter of *if* but *when*. You and your spouse must talk about the boundaries in your marriage and stay true to them.

So what are some ways to safeguard your marriage? Down below, I have listed some rules that we have made in our marriage. You can use these or create your own boundaries to apply specifically to your relationship.

1. Do not take a second look.
2. Never meet with someone of the opposite sex alone.
3. When texting someone of the opposite sex, include your spouse or their spouse.
4. Whenever you feel the enemy is tempting you, you need to flee.
5. Guard your eyes and mind.
6. Be open about your temptations.
7. Never use the D-word.

1. Do not take a second look.

Let's begin with this fact: Attraction is not lust. God made us to be attracted to the opposite sex. It is not a sin to notice a beautiful woman or an attractive man. It is only a sin if we take that attraction to the next step. The sin is not the first look but the second.

Jesus was clear: "You have heard that it was said, 'Do not commit adultery.' But I tell you that anyone who looks at a woman lustfully has already committed adultery with her in his heart" (Matthew 5:27–28 NIV).

Looking lustfully at another person, whether in person or on the internet, on television, or in a magazine, is wrong. We must guard our eyes and ask the Lord to help us when we are tempted. He will always give us a way to escape. God will not let us be tempted beyond our ability to resist, but along with the temptation, He will always provide the way out, so that we will be able to overcome it (1 Corinthians 10:13).

> No temptation [regardless of its source] has overtaken or enticed you that is not common to human experience [nor is any temptation unusual or beyond human resistance]; but God is faithful [to His word—He is compassionate and trustworthy], and He will not let you be tempted beyond your ability [to resist], but along with the temptation He [has in the past and is now and] will [always] provide the way out as well, so that you will be able to endure it [without yielding, and will overcome temptation with joy]. (1 Corinthians 10:13 AMP)

Why is lust wrong? James, the half-brother of Jesus, knew the answer: "Then, after desire has conceived, it gives birth to sin; and sin, when it is full-grown, gives birth to death" (James 1:15 NIV). Everything begins with a thought. Sin always begins in the mind first. When we begin to lust, it will lead us to a path of sin. It never stops with a second look. It did not for David, who was a "man after God's own heart," and it won't stop for you either. I am not saying that you will end up committing adultery, but it can lead to other sins if the lust is not addressed.

King David lusted after Bathsheba when he saw her bathing from the roof of his palace (2 Samuel 11:2). Rather than fleeing from sexual temptation after he saw her beautiful body, he acted on his lust. In verse 3, it says that David sent someone to find out about her. Even though he found out that she was the wife of Uriah the Hittite, David still sent messengers to get her. She came to him, and he slept with her (v. 4). The woman conceived and sent word to David, saying, "I am pregnant" (v. 5). Not only did David commit adultery, but then he had her husband, Uriah, murdered on the battlefield to try to cover up his sin. One sin will always lead to another. What David had done displeased the Lord (v. 27).

> Sin will always take you further than you wanted to go, keep you longer than you wanted to stay, and cost you more than you wanted to pay.
>
> —Ravi Zacharias

So how do we win this battle over sexual temptation? We live in a world where we are bombarded with sexual temptations. You cannot even watch regular television, go to a movie, or be on social media without your eyes being exposed to things that would tempt you sexually. Be on guard and expect to be tempted. Have an escape plan for when temptations arise. Turn the TV off, stop scrolling on the internet, block sites or people, and turn to God in prayer when tempted to take a second glance. Do not just keep looking. If you think that it is not a big deal to look lustfully, then you will become desensitized to the Holy Spirit's conviction and ignore the warning signs when you may be headed down a slippery slope.

> For all that is in the world—the lust of the flesh, the lust of the eyes, and the pride of life—is not of the Father but is of the world. (1 John 2:16 NKJV)

You must renew your mind with the Word of God (see Romans 12:2) each day, so you will not desire the things of the flesh but will walk by the Spirit. When you walk by the Spirit, you will not gratify the desires of the flesh (Galatians 5:16).

> And do not be conformed to this world [any longer with its superficial values and customs], but be transformed and progressively changed [as you mature spiritually] by the renewing of your mind [focusing on godly values and ethical attitudes], so that you may prove [for yourselves] what the will of God is, that which is good and acceptable and perfect [in His plan and purpose for you]. (Romans 12:2 AMP)

To renew our minds each day, we must read and know the Word of God. For the Word of God *is* living and powerful, and sharper than any two-edged sword, piercing even to the division of soul and spirit, and of joints and marrow, and is a discerner of the thoughts and intents of the heart (Hebrews 4:12 NKJV). God speaks to us through His Word. He will instruct, convict, lead, and guide us through His Word. God's Word is powerful, and it is how we defeat the enemy. When we do not know the truth of God's Word, we create a landing strip for the enemy to come and deceive us with his lies. The Word is our sword (see Ephesians 6:17). The sword of the Spirit is the only offensive weapon in the believer's armor (see Ephesians 6:10–18). This weapon is not necessarily the Bible as a whole, but the specific Word that needs to be prayed in a specific situation. How did Jesus overcome Satan's temptations when He was tempted in the wilderness (see Matthew 4:1–11, Luke 4:1–13)? He spoke the Word of God. He said, "It is written …"

Satan Tempts Jesus

Then Jesus, being filled with the Holy Spirit, returned from the Jordan and was led by the Spirit into the wilderness, being tempted for forty days by the devil. And in those days, He ate nothing, and afterward, when they had ended, He was hungry. And the devil said to Him, "If You are the Son of God, command this stone to become bread. But Jesus answered him, saying, "It is written, 'Man shall not live by bread alone, but by every word of God.'"

Then the devil, taking Him up on a high mountain, showed Him all the kingdoms of the world in a moment of time. And the devil said to Him, "All this authority I will give You, and their glory; for this has been delivered to me, and I give it to whomever I wish. Therefore, if You will worship before me, all will be Yours." And Jesus answered and said to him, "Get behind Me, Satan! For it is written, 'You shall worship the LORD your God, and Him only you shall serve.'" Then he brought Him to Jerusalem, set Him on the pinnacle of the temple, and said to Him, "If You are the Son of God, throw Yourself down from here. For it is written: 'He shall give His angels charge over you, to keep you,' and 'In their hands they shall bear you up, lest you dash your foot against a stone.'" And Jesus answered and said to him, "It has been said, 'You shall not tempt the LORD your God.'" Now when the devil had ended every temptation, he departed from Him until an opportune time. (Luke 4:1–13 NKJV)

The most effective thing that we can do when we are tempted is to take it to God immediately and pray the Word of God. Do not try to overcome it with your own willpower and strength because you will fail. In fact, the more you tell yourself not to do something, the stronger that desire becomes. It is like pouring gasoline on the temptation. What you need to do is admit to God that you do not have the strength to defeat the sin on your own and ask for His help.

Refocus your eyes on Jesus. The more you look at Jesus, the less you will be tempted to sin. Pick up your sword (Word of God). Declare that "no temptation has overtaken you except such as is common to man; but God is faithful, who will not allow you to be tempted beyond what you are able, but with the temptation will also make the way of escape, that you may be able to bear it" (1 Corinthians 10:13 NKJV).

We cannot prevent the first look, but we can prevent the second. I encourage you to think of the three areas where you are most tempted. Write down scriptures to memorize and pray whenever you are tempted in those areas. We can overcome the enemy's temptations through the Word of God; prayer, praise, and worship; the name of Jesus; the blood of Jesus; and the cross of Christ. The devil has been rendered powerless by what Jesus did for us on the cross. Remind him of that the next time that he comes to try to tempt you.

> You cannot keep birds from flying over our head, but you can keep them from nesting in your hair.
>
> —Martin Luther

Martin Luther said, "You cannot keep birds from flying over your head, but you can keep them from building a nest in your hair." You can't keep the devil from suggesting thoughts in your mind, but you can choose to not dwell or act on them.

It is also important to confess your sins to each other and pray for one another so that you may be healed. The prayer of a righteous man is powerful and effective (James 5:16). If you are struggling or feeling weak in this area, then confess it to a trustworthy person, who will pray for you and help hold you accountable.

2. Never meet with someone of the opposite sex alone.

Once I owned my own fitness business and began doing ministry, some of the greatest wisdom that I received from our pastors was to never meet with someone of the opposite sex alone. This piece of advice has been crucial to guarding our marriage. It is not that I do not trust myself or that I don't trust the other person; it's Satan that I don't trust, and I know that he will use anything to try to destroy a marriage. I see married people all the time having "business" lunches alone with someone of the opposite sex. If you need to meet with someone, just take another person with you or have your meeting over the phone. It helps to prevent any temptations that could arise. After all, affairs don't start in the bedroom—they start with a conversation. Do not give the devil a foothold. Safeguard your marriage and value your spouse enough to not meet alone with someone of the opposite sex.

3. When texting the opposite sex, include your spouse or their spouse.

When you need to text a person of the opposite sex, again, safeguard your marriage by either including your spouse or their spouse in the text. If this is not an option, then openly share the conversation with your spouse. My husband and I do not hide anything from each other and allow each other to see the messages that we send or receive. There are many times when I need to text someone either for business or ministry and I value my marriage and their marriage enough that I will include either my husband or their wife in the conversation. It is a way to not only show honor but also to show the devil that you are not giving him any access to your marriage.

I remember a time when a married man who was going through a divorce started texting me. He was sharing his problems since I knew his wife and wanted advice. Sounds innocent, right? It always looks innocent, but when you open the door just a little bit, the enemy will try to blow that door wide open. Just a few texts back to try to give encouragement and advice led to this man texting more and more. I told my husband right away, and we prayed about it. The next time that I replied to this man, I added my husband to the thread, and guess what, he stopped texting me. I do not know what his intentions were, and I honestly do not think that he meant any harm, but I safeguarded my marriage to stop any of the enemy's intentions and plans.

I have watched people go through affairs because of them just "talking" with someone of the opposite sex and telling them all their problems. They formed an emotional bond, and their loneliness/hurt landed them in bed with each other. Never talk to someone of the opposite sex about your struggling marriage. Either see a counselor together or talk with someone of the same sex to get the counseling that you need. You may think that it is not a big deal and that it is innocent, but I have witnessed it happen over and over in marriages. All the enemy needs is a little crack in the door, and he will come in to wreak havoc. It is better to be guarded than to be oblivious. Do not be ignorant of the devil's schemes.

> To keep Satan from taking advantage of us; for we are not ignorant of his schemes. (2 Corinthians 2:11 AMP)

If you or your spouse have gone through an affair, my heart breaks for you. The shame, hurt, and betrayal can run deep. I have ministered to many individuals who have gone through an affair, and it is devastating. I have seen many marriages torn apart by it, but I have also seen God bring a beautiful story of healing and restoration. No marriage is too far gone for God. He is the miracle worker, and He can perform a miracle in your marriage. Give God the broken pieces and trust Him to put it all back together.

4. Whenever you feel the enemy is tempting you, you need to flee.

As soon as you feel the enemy is tempting you in any way, the first thing you need to do is *flee*. This is exactly what Joseph did when he was tempted by Potiphar's wife. When we look at the life of Joseph in the Bible, we can see that he was a very honorable and faithful man. Joseph was sold into slavery by his own brothers and taken to Egypt to serve Potiphar, where he found favor in his sight. He then became an overseer of Potiphar's house and had authority over everything he had (Genesis 39:5).

The Bible says that Joseph was handsome in form and appearance (v. 6). Potiphar's wife cast longing eyes on Joseph and wanted him to lie with her, but he refused (vv. 7–8). She did this day by day, but he would not give in to her (v. 10). Still another time, Joseph went into the house to do his work and none of the men of the house were inside (v. 11). Potiphar's wife caught Joseph by his garment, saying, "Lie with me." But he left his garment in her hand and *fled* (v. 12). Joseph could have easily given in to temptation, especially since Potiphar's wife tempted him day after day. But he resisted, fled, and withdrew from the situation.

When you feel tempted, remember what Joseph did. Resist and flee! The Bible says to submit to God, resist the devil, and he will flee from us (James 4:7 NKJV). When we are submitted to God, we can take the authority that we have through Christ Jesus. We can resist the devil, and he must flee from us. Anytime that the enemy is attacking me, I will pray this verse. Study it, memorize it, and use it whenever you face temptations.

5. Guard your eyes and mind.

I believe that one of the biggest open doors to infidelity in a marriage is pornography. When you open this door to the devil, he will blow it wide open and cause destruction. I have watched so many marriages fail due to this open door.

> Flee sexual immorality. Every sin that a man does is outside the body, but he who commits sexual immorality sins against his own body. (1 Corinthians 6:18 NKJV)

Sexual temptation is destructive. Every sin a person commits is outside of the body, but the immoral person sins against his own body. It is a sin against our mind, body, and spirit. It binds, traps, wounds, and kills. It is so powerful. We are not called to fight or resist it. We are simply called to *flee* from it. If we are going to have victory against sexual temptation, we must guard our eyes.

To guard our eyes, we must recognize the power and impact of the images we view and the words we read. The eyes are the doorway to the mind, and whatever one's mind continually thinks about, one will eventually do. If a person is going to be pure, they must be intentional about guarding their eyes. This will affect the types of movies watched, books read, and internet sites visited. When perverse images are continually viewed, a person's lust can become out of control and lead to many sexual sins.

Conversely, a person whose eyes are continually engaging with the Word of God will have the fruit of the Spirit in their lives, which includes love, joy, peace, and self-control (see Galatians 5:22–23). We can keep ourselves pure by reading and obeying God's Word.

> How can a young man keep his way pure? By keeping watch [on himself] according to Your word [conforming his life to Your precepts]. (Psalm 119:9 AMP)

To guard our eyes, we must learn how to *bounce* them. When seeing an attractive person, instead of cultivating lustful thoughts and intentions, quickly bounces your eyes to something else. When seeing seductive images on TV or the internet, instead of taking a second look, bounce your eyes by switching the channel or closing the webpage.

We must guard not only our eyes but also our minds. The mind is very powerful. It is the battlefield. There is a quote that says, "Where the mind goes, the man will follow." Satan loves to put wrong thoughts into our minds—thoughts that are not in agreement with God's Word—hoping we will dwell on them long enough for them to become reality in our lives. The Bible says to take captive every thought to make it obedient to Christ (2 Corinthians 10:5). When the enemy tries to tempt us with the wrong thoughts, instead of dwelling on them, we can take them captive and make them obedient to Christ.

The best way to overcome a wrong thought is to replace it with the Word of God. If you try to tell yourself to stop having that thought, it will only get stronger. You must take the thought captive and then replace it with the truth of God's Word. Only God's Word has the power to help you overcome negative thoughts. Whatever area you are struggling in, find a scripture verse to stand on. Read it, memorize it, and pray it anytime that you are tempted, and God will help you to overcome.

> The weapons of our warfare are not physical [weapons of flesh and blood]. Our weapons are divinely powerful for the destruction of fortresses. We are destroying sophisticated arguments and every exalted and proud thing that sets itself up against the [true] knowledge of God, and we are taking every thought and purpose captive to the obedience of Christ. (2 Corinthians 10:4–5 AMP)

> Finally, believers, whatever is true, whatever is honorable and worthy of respect, whatever is right and confirmed by God's word, whatever is pure and wholesome, whatever is lovely and brings peace, whatever is admirable and of good repute; if there is any excellence, if there is anything worthy of praise, think continually on these things [center your mind on them, and implant them in your heart]. (Philippians 4:8 AMP)

6. Be open about your temptations.

Whatever is hidden has power over us. There is so much freedom once we bring our hidden struggles and sins to the light. James 5:16 (NLT) says, "Confess your sins to each other and pray for each other so that you may be healed. The earnest prayer of a righteous person has great power and produces wonderful results." When we are open and confess our temptations or sins to each other, we can pray for one another, be healed, and set free. Hallelujah!

If you are not at a place where you can be vulnerable and share your temptations with your spouse, then find a trusted source who can help pray for you and keep you accountable.

I have watched so many couples open the door to the temptations in their lives, and then Satan comes in and destroys their marriage. What seemed like something so small ended up becoming a big stronghold. There is an old saying that goes, "Don't play with fire unless you're willing to get burned."

The enemy knows our weaknesses. He preys on them and will try to catch us in our weak moments. Your struggle is different than my struggle. What tempts me is probably not the same as what tempts you. Know what your weaknesses are and share them with someone who can pray for you.

Generally, men are more visual, so they tend to struggle with lust, although women do as well. Physical attraction is more of a temptation for men. My husband was honest and once told me that if we are not intimate as often, it seems that the temptation to look at other women is greater than if we were to be intimate more often. Ladies, do not deprive your men of being intimate with you. I know some women withhold from their husbands as a form of control and manipulation. You are not helping your husband at all by withholding from him. It will only make his temptations greater. Do your part by meeting your husband's physical needs so he is not tempted to look elsewhere.

Please hear my heart … If your spouse has had an affair, my heart goes out to you. Just know that I am not blaming you at all. I know there are many spouses who have taken care of their husband's or wife's physical needs and yet they still cheated on them because of their own issues with lust. If your spouse struggles with lust, pray for them. Do your part to meet their needs, and let God handle the rest.

7. Never use the D-word.

If you want to know what direction your life is going, just listen to the words that you are speaking. There is power in our words. Proverbs 18:21 (ESV) says, "Death and life are in the power of the tongue, and those who love it will eat its fruits." Change your words and change your life!

Early on in our marriage, my husband and I used to throw the "divorce" word around so flippantly, not realizing the damaging effects that it was having. We almost got divorced a couple of times until we finally decided that we had made our vows and we were sticking to them. We made a rule in our marriage that we would not use the word "divorce" ever again. It is amazing what happens when you start *speaking life* over your marriage rather than death and destruction. Ever since we stopped using the big D-word, our marriage has gotten better and stronger and continues to grow.

I want to encourage you to repent for any negative words that you have spoken over your marriage. Do not give the enemy power over your relationship by the negative words that you have spoken out. Start speaking *life* and see your marriage turn around!

> Death and life are in the power of the tongue, And those who love it and indulge it will eat its fruit and bear the consequences of their words. (Proverbs 18:21 AMP)

Remember, if we do not safeguard our marriage by keeping the doors closed to the enemy, then he will come to destroy it. Talk with your spouse and set boundaries to keep your marriage pure so that it will last and not be destroyed by the evil one. What God has joined together, let no man separate (Mark 10:9).

> Therefore what God has joined together, let not man separate. (Mark 10:9 NKJV)

Summary

- We must guard our eyes and ask the Lord to help us when we are tempted.
- Safeguard your marriage and value your spouse enough to not meet alone with someone of the opposite sex.
- All the enemy needs is a little crack in the door, and he will come in to wreak havoc. It is better to be guarded than to be oblivious. Do not be ignorant of the devil's schemes.

- As soon as you feel the enemy is tempting you in any way, the first thing you need to do is *flee*.
- Only God's Word has the power to overcome negative thoughts.
- Whatever is hidden has power over us. There is so much freedom once we bring our hidden struggles and sins to the light.
- If you want to know what direction your life is going, just listen to the words that you are speaking. There is power in our words.

Questions

1. How is the Holy Spirit speaking to me through this chapter?

2. How can we safeguard our marriage? What boundaries need to be set?

3. What are some "cracks" or "open doors" that we have in our marriage? How can we shut these doors to the enemy? What do we need to repent of?

4. Am I speaking positive words about my life and my marriage? Do I need to repent of any negative words that I have spoken?

Prayer

Heavenly Father, help me and my spouse safeguard our marriage. Show us any open door that needs to be shut. Help us to turn away from anything ungodly and walk upright with You. Show us the boundaries that need to be set so that we can keep our marriage pure. What You have joined together, let no man separate in Jesus's name. Amen.

CHAPTER 8

Fighting Fair

It is an honor for a man to keep away from strife [by handling situations with thoughtful foresight], but any fool will [start a] quarrel [without regard for the consequences].

—Proverbs 20:3 (AMP)

News flash! You and your spouse are not going to agree on everything. There will be misunderstandings. Occasional conflicts and disagreements are a part of every relationship, but constant fighting with your spouse is stressful and unhealthy. A pattern of fighting can lead to toxic and harmful behavior that could ultimately end your relationship. If it feels as though you and your spouse are always fighting, it is not too late to change. My husband and I can testify that you can learn to stop fighting and learn how to communicate with each other in a healthy way.

Behind every quarrel is selfishness and pride. James 4:1–4 (NLT) says, "What is causing the quarrels and fights among you? Don't they come from the evil desires at war within you? You want what you do not have, so you scheme and kill to get it. You are jealous of what others have, but you can't get it, so you fight and wage war to take it away from them. Yet you don't have what you want because you don't ask God for it. And even when you ask, you don't get it because your motives are all wrong—you want only what will give you pleasure."

If we truly look behind every quarrel, we will see that the root is our own selfishness and pride. We are selfish beings. It takes dying to our selfish nature *daily* to overcome the quarreling and fighting. Quarrels are fueled by pride, by needing to be right, wanting our way, or by defending our egos. If we were to stop and truly check our motives each time we were about to quarrel, we would see that most likely, it was because we didn't get what we wanted or because things didn't go our way.

> Through pride and presumption come nothing but strife,
> but [skillful and godly] wisdom is with those who welcome
> [well-advised] counsel. (Proverbs 13:10 AMP)

Wisdom resides with those who take advice—those who listen and learn, those who allow themselves to be instructed. There is wisdom in those who humble themselves, who set aside their own selfish ambition, who listen to the other person's point of view, and who allow their own ideas to be corrected. The Bible says in James 4:6 (NKJV), "But He gives more grace. Therefore, He says: 'God resists the proud, but gives grace to the humble.'" When we are walking in pride and stirring up strife, God will resist us, and things will not go well, but when we humble ourselves, we will receive God's grace.

> He who is of a proud heart stirs up strife, but he who trusts in the LORD will be prospered. (Proverbs 28:25 NKJV)

The dictionary defines *strife* as "bickering, arguing, a heated disagreement, or an angry undercurrent." Strife is a trap that the devil lays to destroy marriages, businesses, and even churches. The enemy loves to stir up strife among us because he knows that once we open that door, he can come in to steal, kill, and destroy (see John 10:10). Strife can open the door for every kind of wickedness and prevent us from experiencing God's blessing in our lives. We must peel the curtain back and see how the enemy is at work in our lives.

> The beginning of strife is like letting out water [as from a small break in a dam; first it trickles and then it gushes]; therefore, abandon the quarrel before it breaks out and tempers explode. (Proverbs 17:14 AMP)

God created us to have relationships. The most important relationship is the one we have with Him through our faith in Christ Jesus. When we have a healthy, personal, intimate connection with God, we can have great relationships with the people in our lives.

It is God's will for us to live in peace and harmony with each other. 1 Peter 3:11 (AMP) says, "We must search for peace (with God, with self, with others) and pursue it eagerly (actively—not merely desiring it)." Having peace with others does not mean we will not ever disagree, but we must do it respectfully to avoid strife. You cannot create chaos in the lives of others and expect peace to come into your life. God's presence and blessing dwell where there is unity, not strife.

> If possible, as far as it depends on you, live at peace with everyone. (Romans 12:18 AMP)

So then, let us pursue (with enthusiasm) the things which make for peace and the building up of one another (things which lead to spiritual growth). (Romans 14:19 AMP)

Behold, how good and how pleasant it is for brothers to dwell together in unity! It is like the precious oil [of consecration] poured on the head, coming down on the beard, even the beard of Aaron, coming down upon the edge of his [priestly] robes [consecrating the whole body]. It is like the dew of [Mount] Hermon coming down on the hills of Zion; for there the LORD has commanded the blessing: life forevermore. (Psalm 133:1–3 AMP)

Galatians 5:14–15 (NLT) says, "For the whole law can be summed up in this one command: 'Love your neighbor as yourself.' But if you are always biting and devouring one another, watch out! Beware of destroying one another."

Love is the antidote to strife. Proverbs 10:12 (ESV) says, "Hatred stirs up strife, but love covers all offenses." Love covers a multitude of sins (1 Peter 4:8). It is amazing how strife fizzles out when love is in operation. Choose to overlook an offense and instead walk in love. Just as love is a choice, so is offense and strife.

Good sense and discretion make a man slow to anger, and it is his honor and glory to overlook a transgression or an offense [without seeking revenge and harboring resentment]. (Proverbs 19:11 AMP)

We must learn to stop fighting against each other (because that is what Satan wants us to do) and start fighting together (against the enemy). Kick the enemy out of your home by submitting yourselves to God, resisting the devil, and he will flee (James 4:7). Mark 3:24–25 says, "If a kingdom is divided against itself, that kingdom cannot stand. And if a house is divided against itself, that house cannot stand." A house full of strife will not stand!

A hot-tempered man stirs up strife, but he who is slow to anger and patient calms disputes. (Proverbs 15:18 AMP)

So how do we handle disagreements in a healthy way? Do we just "stuff" everything and not confront the issues in our marriage? No, absolutely not. If we never talk about the issues that arise, they will only lead to bitterness, resentment, and anger. There is a healthy way to confront the conflicts in our marriages. I am all about dealing with issues and confronting them when they arise. I like to nip them in the bud so that they do not have time to build and fester into something greater. My husband and I *talk* about issues now instead of *fighting* about them. There is a difference. Talking requires a calm attitude, whereas fighting is expressed through our emotions.

If you find yourself getting angry, the best thing to do is to walk away from the situation and let your emotions subside. Let your emotions simmer down before you discuss an issue with your spouse. When we are being controlled by our emotions, we will not be able to think clearly or do what God would want us to do in the situation. I used to just react to everything and allow my emotions to dictate how I responded. Now, instead of reacting, I choose to respond.

Reacting is an instinctive, emotional response to a situation. It is often impulsive and can be influenced by our past experiences and fears. On the other hand, *responding* is a thoughtful and deliberate action. It involves considering the situation, weighing the options, and making a conscious decision. We cannot control others' behavior, but we can control ours and how we respond.

After allowing your emotions to subside, pray for wisdom on how to approach and handle the situation. When we ask for wisdom, God will freely give it to us.

> If any of you lacks wisdom, let him ask of God, who gives
> to all liberally and without reproach, and it will be given
> to him. (James 1:5 NKJV)

Once you have the wisdom from God on how to confront an issue, the tone that you use is so important. If you approach your spouse with a defensive tone, then they will be defensive as well. If you use a harsh tone, then it will stir up anger and fuel an argument. The Bible says in Proverbs 15:1 (ESV), "A soft answer turns away wrath, but a harsh word stirs up anger." The way we approach the issue and the tone we use has everything to do with how it will be handled.

We should also approach the issue to find a resolution or solution. As a business owner, I do not like to hear people complaining about something unless they are bringing the issue to my attention to find a solution. We should never be complaining or fighting one another just to hear ourselves complain and fight. If you cannot say anything positive, then do not say anything at all.

> Do all things without complaining and disputing, that you may become blameless and harmless, children of God without fault in the midst of a crooked and perverse generation, among whom you shine as lights in the world. (Philippians 2:14–15 NKJV)

For many years, I had this scripture verse (Philippians 2:14) hanging in my kitchen so that every day I would be reminded not to complain. Our flesh may love to complain, but God hates it. Complaining is a sin. It is certainly not a fruit of the Spirit (Galatians 5:22–23). In fact, it is detrimental to the peace, joy, and patience that come from the Spirit. As believers, we are challenged not to grumble or complain (Philippians 2:14–15, 1 Peter 4:9); rather, we are to love one another deeply so that we may become "blameless and pure" in God's eyes. A complaining spirit leads to fighting and quarreling because complaints come from unfulfilled desires, which lead to envy and strife. The Lord was displeased with the Israelites complaining (Numbers 11:1), and we can be assured that He is displeased with our complaints as well. If I find myself complaining, I ask myself this question, "Am I going to complain about it or pray about it?" I know that I'm only going to get a solution if I pray about it rather than complain about it.

> Now when the people complained, it displeased the LORD; for the LORD heard it, and His anger was aroused. So the fire of the LORD burned among them, and consumed some in the outskirts of the camp. (Numbers 11:1 NKJV)

Ladies, if we have a complaining spirit, it will only lead to us becoming a quarreling wife. I know this for a fact because for many years, I was one! But thank God, through his grace and mercy, He has helped me overcome being the nagging wife and turn into a praising wife. Thank you, Lord! I used to complain to my husband for not taking out the trash. Now I kindly ask him to take it out, or I do it myself. It used to bother me how messy his truck and shed were, but I do not allow it to steal my peace anymore and will make a polite comment about how it looks like he could spend some time organizing/cleaning whenever he has a free moment. God had to deal with me on how I approached my husband and the words and the tone that I was using. It is amazing how our spouse will respond if we approach the situation humbly and with kindness.

The Bible has a lot to say about a quarreling wife. These scriptures may sound harsh, but they are the truth. Allow this truth to sink in and set you free. "Then you will know the truth and the truth will set you free" (John 8:32 NIV).

> A foolish (ungodly) son is destruction to his father, and the contentions of a [quarrelsome] wife are like a constant dripping [of water]. (Proverbs 19:13 AMP)

> It is better to live in a corner of the housetop [on the flat roof, exposed to the weather] than in a house shared with a quarrelsome (contentious) woman. (Proverbs 21:9 AMP)

> It is better to dwell in a desert land than with a contentious and troublesome woman. (Proverbs 21:19 AMP)

> A constant dripping on a day of steady rain and a contentious (quarrelsome) woman are alike; Whoever attempts to restrain her [criticism] might as well try to stop the wind, and grasps oil with his right hand. (Proverbs 27:15–16 AMP)

A quarrelsome wife nags and devalues her husband as a man using negative words. She tears down the very man who is designed to lead, protect, and provide for her and her family. She is always in his face about how he ought to do more, do better, be better, but then is never satisfied with his efforts.

Just like a slow dripping of water through a roof eventually soaks and rots the boards underneath, so does a quarrelsome wife wear down a marriage. She slowly but surely saturates her husband's heart with anger, disappointment, and incompetent feelings, assuring him of failure, and emasculating him one word at a time until he comes to complete ruin. That is a quarrelsome wife—a wife that you do not want to be.

A wife's words of affirmation are huge to her man. Ladies, we can either make or break our husbands. When we lift others up with our words and help them rise, that is when we rise. But if we push others down with our words, you better believe that we are going down with them. We will reap whatever we sow!

> Do not be deceived, God is not mocked; for whatever a man sows, that he will also reap. For he who sows to his flesh will of the flesh reap corruption, but he who sows to the Spirit will of the Spirit reap everlasting life. And let us not grow weary while doing good, for in due season we shall reap if we do not lose heart. (Galatians 6:7–9 NKJV)

Instead of being a nagging wife, we should strive to be a Proverbs 31 wife. This woman provides an excellent example for Christian women to follow today. The Proverbs 31 woman is a woman of wisdom. With God as her guiding source, she has clarity on the decisions she makes, how she lives her life, and the words that she chooses. She speaks with wisdom, and faithful instruction is on her tongue. This virtuous woman works willingly and does not eat the bread of idleness. Instead, she stays busy living out God's purpose for her life each day. She takes care of her household and responsibilities, prioritizing them, even if it means going before her own wants. This noble woman fears the Lord. Her children rise up and call her blessed, and her husband also praises her. While we will never be a perfect woman, we can become the growing, virtuous woman that God created us to be.

Description of a Worthy Woman

An excellent woman [one who is spiritual, capable, intelligent, and virtuous], who is he who can find her? Her value is more precious than jewels and her worth is far above rubies or pearls. The heart of her husband trusts in her [with secure confidence],

And he will have no lack of gain. She comforts, encourages, and does him only good and not evil all the days of her life. She looks for wool and flax and works with willing hands in delight. She is like the merchant ships [abounding with treasure]; She brings her [household's] food from far away. She rises also while it is still night and gives food to her household, and assigns tasks to her maids. She considers a field before she buys or accepts it [expanding her business prudently]; With her profits she plants fruitful vines in her vineyard. She equips herself with strength [spiritual, mental, and physical fitness for her God-given task] and makes her arms strong. She sees that her gain is good; Her lamp does not go out, but it burns continually through the night [she is prepared for whatever lies ahead]. She stretches out her hands to the distaff, And her hands hold the spindle [as she spins wool into thread for clothing].

She opens and extends her hand to the poor, and she reaches out her filled hands to the needy. She does not fear the snow for her household, for all in her household are clothed in [expensive] scarlet [wool]. She makes for herself coverlets, cushions, and rugs of tapestry.

Her clothing is linen, pure and fine, and purple [wool]. Her husband is known in the [city's] gates, when he sits among the elders of the land. She makes [fine] linen garments and sells them; and supplies sashes to the merchants. Strength and dignity are her clothing and her position is strong and secure; and she smiles at the future [knowing that she and her family are prepared]. She opens her mouth in [skillful and godly] wisdom, and the teaching of kindness is on her tongue [giving counsel and instruction]. She looks well to how things go in her household, and does not eat the bread of idleness. Her children rise up and call her blessed (happy, prosperous, to be admired); Her husband also, and he praises her, saying, "Many daughters have done nobly, and well [with the strength of character that is steadfast in goodness], but you excel them all." Charm and grace are deceptive, and [superficial] beauty is vain, but a woman who fears the LORD [reverently worshiping, obeying, serving, and trusting Him with awe-filled respect], she shall be praised. Give her of the product of her hands, and let her own works praise her in the gates [of the city]. (Proverbs 31:10–31 AMP)

One of our rules for when we have a disagreement is to always settle it before the day is over. We never go to bed angry to prevent the issue from festering. We do not want to give the devil any foothold in our marriage with strife, anger, unforgiveness, bitterness, or resentment. My husband and I will humble ourselves and come together to talk about a given issue and pray before going to bed. It is amazing what prayer will do. There have been times when we are still upset and we come together to pray, and suddenly, the feelings of anger just completely dissipate.

God is so faithful to intervene when we include Him and seek His help. We must deal with any anger and not go to bed with it. Ephesians 4:26–27 (AMP) says, "Be angry [at sin—at immorality, at injustice, at ungodly behavior], yet do not sin; do not let your anger [cause you shame, nor allow it to] last until the sun goes down. And do not give the devil an opportunity [to lead you into sin by holding a grudge, or nurturing anger, or harboring resentment, or cultivating bitterness]."

If you are not able to settle an issue with your spouse before you go to bed, then be sure that you get with The Lord and deal with your own heart. You cannot control how your spouse responds, but you can control your own feelings and how you deal with the situation. You may have to put off talking about the issue you are facing until you can both get some rest and have a clear mind, but be sure that you deal with any anger so you can go to bed with peace in your heart. Spending time in the Lord's presence, His Word, and prayer will help you to find peace.

> Be angry [at sin – at immorality, at injustice, at ungodly behavior], yet do not sin; do not let your anger [cause you shame, nor allow it to] last until the sun goes down. And do not give the devil an opportunity [to lead you into sin by holding a grudge, or nurturing anger, or harboring resentment, or cultivating bitterness]. (Ephesians 4:26–27 AMP)

> Let all bitterness and wrath and anger and clamor [perpetual animosity, resentment, strife, fault-finding] and slander be put away from you, along with every kind of malice [all spitefulness, verbal abuse, malevolence]. Be kind and helpful to one another, tender-hearted [compassionate, understanding], forgiving one another [readily and freely], just as God in Christ also forgave you. (Ephesians 4:31–32 AMP)

To have a healthy marriage, we must learn to forgive quickly. Unforgiveness will eat us alive. It is toxic to our bodies. There is an old saying that goes, "Unforgiveness is like drinking poison and expecting the other person to die." It is so true! It slowly kills the one unwilling to forgive another. We must forgive others just as the Lord has forgiven us.

> Bearing graciously with one another, and willingly forgiving each other if one has a cause for complaint against another; just as the Lord has forgiven you, so should you forgive. (Colossians 3:13 AMP)

There is a healthy way to handle conflict in our marriage. When an issue arises, talk about it calmly. If the conversation starts to become heated, one of you should take the higher road and say that you need to allow your emotions to subside before continuing the conversation. Pray and ask God how you should *respond* rather than *reacting* out of your flesh. Satan wants you to

HOW TO TRAIN YOUR SPOUSE

fight and have division in your marriage. You will never defeat the devil with man-made ways (by fighting from your flesh). You defeat the devil by praying scripture. When the devil hits you and your marriage, you hit him back with scripture. Humble yourself and come together with your spouse to talk/pray about the issue, with the intent of finding a resolution, not with an ulterior motive to show that you are right. I heard a wise woman once say, "Give up your right to be right." We should never be fighting to prove that we are right. That's just pride. We are to humble ourselves and work together to find a solution to the problem, even if that means giving up our right to be right. Find scriptures that you can stand on and do not allow the enemy to stir up strife/division in your marriage. Forgive each other, just as the Lord has forgiven you.

Summary

- Occasional conflicts and disagreements are a part of every relationship, but constant fighting with your spouse is stressful and unhealthy.
- When we have a healthy, personal, intimate connection with God, we can have great relationships with the people in our lives.
- You cannot create chaos in the lives of others and expect peace to come into your life. God's presence and blessing dwell where there is unity, not strife.
- Love is the antidote to strife. Proverbs 10:12 (ESV) says, "Hatred stirs up strife, but love covers all offenses."
- We must learn to stop fighting against each other (because that is what Satan wants us to do) and start fighting together (against the enemy). Kick the enemy out of your home by submitting yourselves to God, resisting the devil, and he will flee (James 4:7).
- My husband and I "talk" about issues now instead of "fighting" about them. There is a difference. Talking requires a calm attitude whereas fighting is expressed through our emotions.
- "Unforgiveness is like drinking poison and expecting the other person to die." It is so true! It slowly kills the one unwilling to forgive another. We must forgive others just as the Lord has forgiven us.

Questions

1. How is the Holy Spirit speaking to me through this chapter?

2. Are we handling conflict in a healthy way? Are we *responding* thoughtfully or *reacting* out of our flesh to situations?

3. How can we stop fighting and start communicating in a positive way, working together to resolve the issue?

4. Have I been seeking the Lord when an issue arises? Do I ask for His wisdom? Do I allow Him to deal with my heart?

Prayer

Heavenly Father, please help us to shut the door to strife in our lives. When issues arise, help us to talk through and handle them in a way that honors You. I pray that we stand together and fight the enemy and not allow him to come between us in our marriage. Help us to humble ourselves and respond in the way that You would want us to respond rather than react out of our flesh. I ask this in Jesus's name. Amen.

CHAPTER 9

Love and Forgiveness

So, as God's own chosen people, who are holy [set apart, sanctified for His purpose] and well-beloved [by God Himself], put on a heart of compassion, kindness, humility, gentleness, and patience [which has the power to endure whatever injustice or unpleasantness comes, with good temper]; bearing graciously with one another, and willingly forgiving each other if one has a cause for complaint against another; just as the Lord has forgiven you, so should you forgive. Beyond all these things put on and wrap yourselves in [unselfish] love, which is the perfect bond of unity [for everything is bound together in agreement when each one seeks the best for others].

—Colossians 3:12–14 (AMP)

I know that I have spoken on forgiveness a couple of times already in this book, but I feel that it is a topic that many struggle with and need for their freedom. Unforgiveness will keep us stuck and locked in our own prisons. Not only will it cause us to become bitter and angry, but it can also cause many health and mental problems. Unforgiveness will cause stress, anxiety, depression, insecurity, and a hardened heart. It can also cause sickness and diseases. It will hinder not only your relationship with others but also your fellowship with God.

Since the cross of Christ boldly proclaims the love and forgiveness of God, how could we not forgive others? Are we not called and empowered with the same love and forgiveness that was generously extended to us when we placed our trust in the Lord? Christ's love was so pure that He gave His life for us. "Greater love has no one than this, that someone lay down his life for his friends" (John 15:13 ESV). But there was another gift that Jesus bestowed while He was hanging on the cross, a gift that further measured the magnitude of His great love: He forgave and asked his Father to forgive those who persecuted and crucified Him.

Most likely, none of us will be asked to give up our lives for others, but we will be faced with the challenge of forgiveness. If you have walked this earth for any time at all, you have experienced being hurt by others and tested whether you will forgive. It is not easy to forgive as the hurt and wounds inflicted by others are very real, but forgiveness does not free the other person—it frees us. We get locked inside our own prison when we choose to not forgive.

We do not deserve to be forgiven of our sins, and we cannot do anything to earn it, but Jesus freely gave it to us. What gives us any right to withhold forgiveness from others? I have learned that you cannot give away something that you haven't received for yourself. If you have not received the love and forgiveness from Christ Jesus, then you will not be able to give it to others. I remember many years ago before I had a real relationship with Jesus, when I struggled to forgive others and it was all because I had not understood and received forgiveness for my own sins through Christ Jesus.

Maybe you need to forgive yourself. You may think that you have messed up so badly that God could never forgive you. The devil is a liar! There is nothing that you have done that God will not or cannot forgive.

All you must do is ask Him to forgive you of your sins, and He will forgive you and cleanse you of all unrighteousness. He will also remove the sins as far as the east is from the west.

> If we [freely] admit that we have sinned and confess our sins, He is faithful and just [true to His own nature and promises], and will forgive our sins and cleanse us continually from all unrighteousness [our wrongdoing, everything not in conformity with His will and purpose]. (1 John 1:9 AMP)

> As far as the east is from the west, so far has He removed our transgressions from us. (Psalm 103:12 NKJV)

There is a saying that goes, "It's hard to heal what you won't reveal." Anything hidden in darkness has power over us. When it is brought to the light, we can truly walk in freedom and overcome the powers of darkness. Every hidden thing will eventually manifest, and anything in secret will come to light (Luke 8:17). If you want to walk in freedom, bring the hidden things to light. Confess, repent, and forgive quickly.

> For there is nothing hidden that will not become evident, nor anything secret that will not be known and come out into the open. (Luke 8:17 AMP)

In Matthew 18, Jesus tells a parable of a man who is forgiven an overwhelming financial debt that he owed to a king. However, this same man, who had been shown great mercy, refused to extend the same forgiveness to his servant who owed him a much smaller amount. The unmerciful one even goes to the extreme measure of putting his servant in prison until he can pay the wages that he owes. Jesus goes on to describe the unmerciful man as the one who is tortured because of his unforgiveness. If we do not forgive others when they sin against us, our Heavenly Father will not forgive us (Matthew 6:15). The torture of anger, resentment, and bitterness are all fruits of unforgiveness, while love's healing fruit is forgiveness.

The Parable of the Unforgiving Servant

Then Peter came to Him and said, "LORD, how often shall my brother sin against me, and I forgive him? Up to seven times?" Jesus said to him, "I do not say to you, up to seven times, but up to seventy times seven. Therefore, the kingdom of heaven is like a certain king who wanted to settle accounts with his servants. And when he had begun to settle accounts, one was brought to him who owed him ten thousand talents. But as he was not able to pay, his master commanded that he be sold, with his wife and children and all that he had, and that payment be made. The servant therefore fell down before him, saying, 'Master, have patience with me, and I will pay you all.' Then the master of that servant was moved with compassion, released him, and forgave him the debt. "But that servant went out and found one of his fellow servants who owed him a hundred denarii; and he laid hands on him and took him by the throat, saying, 'Pay me what you owe!' So his fellow servant fell down at his feet and begged him, saying, 'Have patience with me, and I will pay you all.' And he would not, but went and threw him into prison till he should pay the debt. So when his fellow servants saw what had been done, they were very grieved, and came and told their master all that had been done. Then his master, after he had called him, said to him, 'You wicked servant! I forgave you all that debt because you begged me. Should you not also have had compassion on your fellow servant, just as I had pity on you?' And his master was angry, and delivered him to the torturers until he should pay all that was due to him. "So My heavenly Father also will do to you if each of you, from his heart, does not forgive his brother his trespasses." (Matthew 18:21–35 NKJV)

One of the many important aspects of love is forgiveness. In any relationship, if forgiveness is not given and received, the chance of it surviving diminishes. The future of your marriage is often determined by your willingness to let go of the past. Forgiving your spouse means that you can't throw their past mistakes in their face every time you are upset with them. True forgiveness means that you let go of the offense and you move forward, without rehearsing the pain or bringing it up again.

What is forgiveness? Wikipedia defines *forgiveness* as "the intentional and voluntary process by which one who may initially feel victimized, undergoes a change in feelings and attitude regarding a given offense, and overcomes negative emotions such as resentment and vengeance (however justified it might be)." Forgiveness is a voluntary decision, not a feeling.

In every relationship, there are times when we are hurt or disappointed by the other person. When we decide to forgive, we are saying, "I love you regardless of what you did or said." That commitment to the relationship is a choice and a decision to love. We cannot always forgive on our own. Sometimes the hurt is so deep that it takes a supernatural act of God to help us walk through forgiveness. But when we extend forgiveness, it shows others who God is in us. When we choose to walk in love, it shows that we know God. 1 John 4:8 (ESV) says, "Anyone who does not love does not know God, because God is love."

> Beloved, let us love one another, for love is of God; and everyone who loves is born of God and knows God. He who does not love does not know God, for God is love. In this the love of God was manifested toward us, that God has sent His only begotten Son into the world, that we might live through Him. In this is love, not that we loved God, but that He loved us and sent His Son to be the propitiation for our sins. Beloved, if God so loved us, we also ought to love one another. No one has seen God at any time. If we love one another, God abides in us, and His love has been perfected in us. (1 John 4:7–12 NKJV)

> We love Him because He first loved us. If someone says, "I love God," and hates his brother, he is a liar; for he who does not love his brother whom he has seen, how can he love God whom he has not seen? And this commandment

we have from Him: that he who loves God must love his brother also. (1 John 4:19–21 NKJV)

We can never love God or others until we have experienced His love ourselves. The only way that we can truly love and forgive is by receiving the Father's love and forgiveness through Jesus Christ. Open your heart today and freely receive so that you can freely give to others.

If your heart is hardened, then pray this verse (Ezekiel 36:26) over yourself every day. Ask the Lord to soften your heart so that you can extend love and forgiveness to others. Remember, if you do not forgive, then you yourself will not be forgiven. Love and forgiveness are a choice. Will you choose to forgive?

> Moreover, I will give you a new heart and put a new spirit within you, and I will remove the heart of stone from your flesh and give you a heart of flesh. (Ezekiel 36:26 AMP)

Summary

- Unforgiveness will keep us stuck and locked in our own prisons.
- There was another gift that Jesus bestowed while He was hanging on the cross, a gift that further measured the magnitude of His great love: He forgave and asked His Father to forgive those who persecuted and crucified Him.
- Most likely, none of us will be asked to give up our lives for others, but we will be faced with the challenge of forgiveness.
- It is not easy to forgive as the hurt and wounds inflicted by others are very real, but forgiveness does not free the other person—it frees us.
- We do not deserve to be forgiven for our sins, and we cannot do anything to earn it, but Jesus freely gave it to us.
- One of the many important aspects of love is forgiveness. In any relationship, if forgiveness is not given and received, the chance of it surviving diminishes. The future of your marriage is often determined by your willingness to let go of the past.

- The only way that we can truly love and forgive is by receiving the Father's love and forgiveness through Jesus Christ.

Questions

1. How is the Holy Spirit speaking to me through this chapter?

2. Is there any unforgiveness in my heart? Who do I need to forgive? Do I need to forgive my spouse or myself?

3. Is there anything that I am hiding that needs to be brought to the light? What do I need to deal with in my heart?

4. Have I received God's love and forgiveness for myself? Am I extending that same love and forgiveness toward others?

Prayer

Heavenly Father, soften my heart. Show me anyone that I am holding unforgiveness or bitterness toward. Forgive me of my sins and help me to extend that same forgiveness to others. I release anyone who has hurt me. I hold nothing to their charge. I ask You to help me truly forgive them and to bless them. I do not want unforgiveness or bitterness to poison my heart and hold me back anymore. I choose to forgive my spouse for anything that they have done. Cleanse my heart today and bring healing to any wounds. Help me to receive Your love and to love others in Jesus's name. Amen.

CHAPTER 10

Pray about Everything

Again I say to you that if two of you agree on earth concerning anything that they ask, it will be done for them by My Father in heaven. For where two or three are gathered together in My name, I am there in the midst of them.

—Matthew 18:19–20 (NKJV)

Prayer is communion with God. It is a two-way conversation where we not only talk to God, we also listen to what He is saying. There is power in prayer. Nothing happens unless we pray. Prayer has the power to accomplish what nothing else can. People will often say that they are sending positive thoughts or good vibes. Nobody's life was ever changed by positive "vibes" or "thoughts sent your way," but prayer, in Jesus's name, shakes the gates of hell. Things happen when people pray! Our marriages should be a union of prayer.

> Therefore, confess your sins to one another [your false steps, your offenses], and pray for one another, that you may be healed and restored. The heartfelt and persistent prayer of a righteous man (believer) can accomplish much [when put into action and made effective by God—it is dynamic and can have tremendous power]. (James 5:16 AMP)

My marriage changed when we began to pray. I am not talking about the "Bless this food to the nourishment of our bodies" prayer before we eat or any other routine prayer. I am talking about taking each other's hand and praying together for our marriage, our family, every decision we make, and the things that concern us. We also pray for our church, schools, city, nation, and families, or anyone that the Lord puts on our hearts to pray for. We have decided that as a couple, we will not make any big decisions without first praying together. This includes decisions with our family, in our businesses, any opportunities, or large purchases. We will pray and seek the Lord for what He wants us to do. If we are both not in agreement with it, then we will not move forward.

Where there is no peace, we will not proceed. I remember one time when we were praying for a certain construction job for my husband that looked like a great opportunity, but I did not have peace about it. I could not explain why I was out of peace, but we believed that there was a reason. My husband did not accept the job. We later found out that there ended up being a lawsuit with that construction job, and we now know that the Lord was protecting us. It is amazing the clarity, wisdom, and direction that the Lord will give you if you take the time to pray.

Prayer was never meant to be a ritual or something that you just do on Sundays at church. Prayer is a conversation with God—one where you not only talk to Him, you also listen. God speaks to us in many ways—through His Word, worship, dreams, visions, thoughts, nudges, other people, and through the Holy Spirit's still, small voice. It is our Heavenly Father's desire to communicate with Him through prayer.

> Then He said, "Go out, and stand on the mountain before the LORD." And behold, the LORD passed by, and a great and strong wind tore into the mountains and broke the rocks in pieces before the LORD, but the LORD was not in the wind; and after the wind an earthquake, but the LORD was not in the earthquake; and after the earthquake a fire, but the LORD was not in the fire; and after the fire a still small voice. So it was, when Elijah heard it, that he wrapped his face in his mantle and went out and stood in the entrance of the cave. Suddenly a voice came to him, and said, "What are you doing here, Elijah?" (1 Kings 19:11–13 NKJV)

God calls us to pray continually (1 Thessalonians 5:17), be devoted to prayer (Colossians 4:2), and pray in the Spirit on all occasions with all kinds of prayers and requests (Ephesians 6:18). Prayer should not be ignored; it needs to be part of our lives each day. In Romans 12:12 (NIV), the apostle Paul tells us to "be joyful in hope, patient in affliction, faithful in prayer." Clearly, prayer is important to God, which is why Jesus taught us how to pray with the Lord's Prayer.

> In this manner, therefore, pray:
> Our Father in heaven,
> Hallowed be Your name.
> Your kingdom come.
> Your will be done
> On earth as it is in heaven.
> Give us this day our daily bread.
> And forgive us our debts,
> As we forgive our debtors.
> And do not lead us into temptation,
> But deliver us from the evil one.

For Yours is the kingdom and the power and the glory
forever. Amen.
(Matthew 6:9–13 NKJV)

Jesus gave us this model so we would know how to pray. It teaches us
six unique steps to guide us in prayer.

1. Address God appropriately as our Father, who is holy.
2. Praise God for who He is and what He has done.
3. Submit to His will being done in our lives.
4. Ask God for what we need—our daily bread.
5. Confess how we have sinned and repent with a humble heart.
6. Request God's protection to overcome the evil one's temptations
    and attacks on our lives.

Daily prayer can bless you, your family, and those you pray for. Every
day, I encourage you to spend time with God to pray and allow Him to
speak to you. Open the Bible and read His Word. When you open your
Bible, God will open His mouth and speak to you.

Talk to God about everything. If it concerns you and you care about
it, then God cares about it too. There is nothing too big or too small for
God. Cast your cares upon Him through prayer.

Casting all your care upon Him, for He cares for you.
(1 Peter 5:7 NKJV)

Prayer works because God wants our complete dependence on Him. He
is and wants us to make Him the answer to our longings. God is the source
of our fulfillment. Prayer draws us into a deep relationship with God. Our
prayer life brings us closer to Him through honest communication, just
as any child does with their parents. Deep, intimate prayer draws us close
to the heart of God. It helps us to become more like Him. Prayer lets us
hear the Father's voice and direction. It gives us clarity and answers. As we
share our deepest longings with God, we change and become the people
God wants us to be.

While God will always answer our prayers, He may not answer them
in the way that we expect, or think is best, or on our timetable. I have

learned that God's timing is not the same as my timing. Sometimes God says "Yes" to our prayers, sometimes he says "No," and often he says "Wait." But we must trust God's will, for He truly knows what is best for us. I remember when everything seemed to be falling apart in a certain aspect of my life. I asked the Lord what was happening. He said to me, "I am answering your prayers. It is just not the way that you thought it would be."

I can look back now and see how God answered my prayers and delivered me out of a situation. It just looked completely different than how I thought it should be. God's thoughts are not our thoughts, and His ways are not our ways. His thoughts and ways are so much higher than ours. Aren't you thankful for that? Our finite minds cannot possibly understand an infinite God.

> "For My thoughts are not your thoughts, nor are your ways My ways," says the LORD. "For as the heavens are higher than the earth, so are My ways higher than your ways, and My thoughts than your thoughts." (Isaiah 55:8–9 NKJV)

We must pray for our marriages through the ups and downs and stay committed to each other, just as we vowed, in good times and bad. We should pray for our marriages when things are going well and when times are tough. We pray when we feel like praying, and especially in those times that we do not feel like praying. Prayer connects us not only to God but also to each other. Praying with your spouse is one of the most intimate things you can do with them. Research shows that couples who pray together have an increase in trust and unity, relationship satisfaction and commitment, and a decrease in infidelity. Prayer is one of the most powerful ways that we can fight for our marriages. I encourage you to pray *with* your spouse and *for* your spouse each day.

A prayer to pray with your spouse:

Heavenly Father, thank You for the gift of marriage. Thank You for joining our hearts together. We pray that what You have joined together, let no man separate (Mark 10:9). Help us to put You first in our marriage and in our lives. May we honor You by the way that we love and treat each other. Help us to walk in humility and consider one another more important than ourselves (Philippians 2:3). Teach us how to see through Your eyes of love. We pray that we will be kind and tenderhearted, forgiving each other just as You have forgiven us (Ephesians 4:32). Help our marriage to grow and be a reflection of You in Jesus's mighty name. Amen.

A prayer to pray for your spouse:

Heavenly Father, thank You for the spouse that You have blessed me with. I lift them up to You right now and ask that You bless them. I pray that You will cause them to be prosperous with the work of their hands (Deuteronomy 30:9). Fill them with all wisdom and discernment. Help them to follow Your ways and be led by the Holy Spirit. May they walk by the Spirit so they will not gratify the desires of the flesh (Galatians 5:16). I plead the precious blood of Jesus over them and pray for protection in every area of their life. Guard them from any temptations and help them turn to You whenever they are tempted so You will give them a way out (1 Corinthians 10:13). Strengthen them where they are weak and help them to become the person that You created them to be. Guard their mind and their heart. I pray that they would fear You Lord and love You with all their heart, all their soul, and all their mind (Matthew 22:37) in Jesus's name. Amen.

Summary

- Prayer is communion with God. It is a two-way conversation where we not only talk to God but also listen to what He is saying.
- Things happen when people pray! Our marriages should be a union of prayer.
- Daily prayer can bless you, your family, and those you pray for. Each day I encourage you to spend time with God to pray and allow Him to speak to you.
- Prayer works because God wants our complete dependence on Him. He is and wants us to make Him the answer to our longings.
- Prayer draws us into a deep relationship with God.

- While God will always answer our prayers, He may not answer them in the way that we expect, or think is best, or on our timetable. I have learned that God's timing is not the same as my timing. Sometimes God says "Yes" to our prayers, sometimes he says "No," and often he says "Wait."

- Praying with your spouse is one of the most intimate things you can do with them. Research shows that couples who pray together have an increase in trust and unity, relationship satisfaction and commitment, and a decrease in infidelity. Prayer is one of the most powerful ways that we can fight for our marriages.

Questions

1. How is the Holy Spirit speaking to me through this chapter?

2. How is my prayer life? How could I improve it? Is my prayer life just a religious routine, or do I have an intimate relationship with God?

3. Do I pray with my spouse? If not, how can we start incorporating prayer into our relationship? If so, how can we better our prayer life together?

4. Do I take the time to listen to God in my prayer time? How do I mostly hear Him speak to me—through His Word, worship, dreams, visions, thoughts, nudges, other people, or through the Holy Spirit's still, small voice?

Prayer

God, thank You for teaching me the importance of prayer. Help me to keep You first in my life and make prayer a priority in my marriage. I want to live a life devoted to You. Teach us how You want us to pray every day by being led by the Holy Spirit. Help me and my spouse come together to pray about everything in Jesus's name. Amen.

CHAPTER 11

Intimacy

But because of [the temptation to participate in] sexual immorality, let each man have his own wife, and let each woman have her own husband. The husband must fulfill his [marital] duty to his wife [with good will and kindness], and likewise the wife to her husband. The wife does not have [exclusive] authority over her own body, but the husband shares with her; and likewise, the husband does not have [exclusive] authority over his body, but the wife shares with him. Do not deprive each other [of marital rights], except perhaps by mutual consent for a time, so that you may devote yourselves [unhindered] to prayer, but come together again so that Satan will not tempt you [to sin] because of your lack of self-control.

—1 Corinthians 7:2–5 (AMP)

I am sure some of you ladies do not like this scripture verse about sexual intimacy (1 Corinthians 7:2–5). God obviously knew that we would need help in this area. He knew that there would be sexual immorality in this world that we live in and wanted to provide us with guidelines on how to stay sexually pure in our marriages. He also knew that we would need to be reminded to take care of our spouse's sexual needs. Sex is God's gift to marriage. Wives, don't turn your noses up on something that God gave you as a gift to be enjoyed with your husband. It seems that people usually do not seem to struggle with sexual intimacy when they first get married, so why do we tend to struggle the longer we have been married?

There are many factors that can lead to a decrease in sexual intimacy within a marriage including busyness, physical exhaustion, hormone fluctuation, menopause, health issues, mental issues, having children, relationship issues, job stress, infidelity, and women not feeling comfortable with their bodies.

For many couples, maintaining intimacy in their relationship can become a challenge over time. The lack of intimacy in a marriage can have profound effects on the emotional and physical well-being of both partners and may even lead to the breakdown of their marriage.

When a woman lacks intimacy in her marriage, it can have a significant impact on her emotional and physical health. The lack of physical touch, emotional connection, and sexual intimacy can lead to feelings of loneliness, depression, and low self-esteem. It can also cause physical symptoms such as headaches, insomnia, and decreased libido. When a woman does not feel emotionally or physically connected to her partner, she may have little interest in sex. This can lead to tension in the relationship and make it difficult for the couple to connect physically. Additionally, the lack of intimacy can create a communication gap, leading to misunderstandings and conflict. My husband and I always know that when we misunderstand each other and start to feel tension, it is time to reconnect physically. It always seems to work!

Intimacy is an essential part of any marriage. It provides a sense of security, love, and acceptance that is critical for a man's and woman's being. When a woman lacks intimacy in a marriage, she may feel undesired and unimportant. A woman needs to feel wanted. Emotional intimacy is an essential part of a healthy marriage. Without an emotional connection, a woman can feel that her partner does not understand her and her needs are not being met. When a woman feels that her partner does not find her attractive, it can lead to a negative body image. Women tend to not want to be intimate if they do not feel good about their bodies. Ladies, even if you do not feel good about yourself, being intimate with your husband will help you to feel good about yourself. There are so many benefits of sex, and one of the great benefits is the hormones that are released after intercourse.

During each sexual encounter, our bodies release the hormone oxytocin, also known as the love hormone. This hormone is responsible for creating feelings of intimacy and bonding between partners. Without intimacy in marriage, it is easy for us to break our connection. Sex fulfills your physical needs and establishes an emotional connection between the two of you. The emotional connection factor is more important for women than for men. The oxytocin hormone can also help reduce symptoms of depression and anxiety and improve overall mood. This is because oxytocin promotes the release of endorphins, which are naturally mood-boosting chemicals in the brain.

Dopamine is another hormone that is released during sexual activity and is associated with pleasure and reward, leading to feelings of euphoria and satisfaction. This hormone is released during pleasurable activities such as eating, exercising, and sexual activity. Dopamine makes you feel happy, motivated, alert, and focused. If you have a high dopamine level, you will feel euphoric, energized, and highly sexually driven. If you have a low dopamine level, you will feel tired, unmotivated, and unhappy. You may also have memory loss, mood swings, and sleeping problems.

Serotonin is the hormone responsible for regulating mood, appetite, sleep, and sexual function. During sexual activity, the release of serotonin in the brain can lead to increased sexual desire and a sense of contentment after sex. This hormone is responsible for good mood, relaxation, and the drowsiness that sets in and makes you want to nap. This is definitely the hormone responsible for putting my husband to sleep in 2.5 seconds after we are intimate with each other.

Research suggests that having frequent sex with our spouse can play a role in a person's overall well-being. The benefits of having sex within your marriage include lowering blood pressure, releasing stress, cutting the risk of cancer (especially prostate cancer in men), improving the immune system, better sleep, driving away depression by releasing serotonin, making you look younger and attractive from the release of a chemical called pheromones, which will increase your appeal, helping you to have more confidence, a better memory, softer skin, as well as promote happiness and make your relationship stronger.

As you can see, there are many benefits to having sex in a marriage. Not only will it benefit you as a couple, but it will also benefit you individually. You will be a healthier and happier person.

When we meet the sexual needs of our spouse, it also helps to safeguard our marriage from sexual immorality. Just like the verse says in 1 Corinthians 7:2-5, we should not deprive one another of sexual relations. Depriving one another will only have a negative impact on our relationship. Plus, we will be missing out on all the other positive benefits.

Infidelity can be a result of a lack of intimacy in a marriage. When a man or a woman does not feel emotionally or physically connected to her partner, he or she may seek intimacy outside of the marriage. This is never the answer. Adultery in a marriage will not only defile the marriage bed, but it will also cause guilt and shame and can ultimately destroy the relationship. If you or your spouse have fallen into infidelity, the first thing to do is repent and turn away from the sin. Repent to your spouse and to God. Ask the Lord to cleanse you of sin and restore your marriage. Pray to break any soul tie that you had with anyone other than your spouse and ask God to purify your relationship.

Married couples must learn to view sex as a way to serve each other and meet each other's needs. Sadly, sex in marriage is often about fulfilling one's lust or reaching one's own climax instead of serving. Consequently, a spouse can feel used or unsatisfied sexually in marriage. This was never God's intended plan. In sex, as with every relationship, nothing should be done out of selfish motivation but primarily to serve the interests of the other. In sex, the husband's goal should be his wife's pleasure, and the wife's goal should be her husband's pleasure.

> Let nothing be done through selfish ambition or conceit,
> but in lowliness of mind let each esteem others better than
> himself. Let each of you look out not only for his own

interests, but also for the interests of others. (Philippians 2:3–4 NKJV)

You may be saying to yourself that you just do not have time. Just like anything else in your life, you must make time. Having five kids, I know how difficult it can be to find time alone with my husband. You either stay up later, wake up earlier, have lunch dates, or make it a weekend date night.

Another excuse you may have had is that you are too physically exhausted. Something I always tell my clients when they are too tired to exercise is, "It takes energy to create energy." If you can just muster up the energy and strength to have sex with your husband, you will then create energy by the positive endorphins that run through your body. It truly is amazing!

Some of you may have no desire whatsoever because you were abused in the past and have a negative experience with sex. If you are one of the many who have been sexually abused, I am so sorry that happened to you. I cannot relate as that is something I have not experienced in my own life, but I cannot even imagine the pain and trauma that it brought to you. I do know that Jesus can heal you of any pain, fear, and trauma that you have experienced. He is our healer, and He can heal anything that we have ever gone through in our lives. I know of several women who were sexually abused and received the healing in their lives that only Jesus can bring. Give your hurts over to God and ask Him to heal you from those traumatic experiences. I pray that He will give you beauty from those ashes (Isaiah 61:3) and help you to have a wonderful sex life with your spouse that can be enjoyed.

If you simply do not enjoy being intimate with your spouse, then maybe it is time to change things up. I think boredom often keeps couples from being sexually intimate with each other. If you are bored, then most likely, your spouse is bored too. Change things up and keep it fresh. You will find that it will bring excitement to you both! Husbands, here is a word of advice for you. Make your wife feel loved and not just a sex object. When you make her feel loved, she will want to be intimate with you. But if you are not showing her love, I can guarantee that she will not want to do anything with you.

Being sexual with your spouse is not the only way to be intimate. We can grow in our intimacy with each other through hugging, kissing, cuddling, flirting, holding hands, massage, prayer, and speaking loving words to each other. I realize that there are some couples who physically cannot be sexually active. If this is the case for you, find other ways to be intimate with each other. If you are struggling in this area of being intimate with your spouse, I encourage you to pray and ask for the Lord's help. He will be faithful to answer your prayers and help you when you call upon Him. Also, do not allow your feelings to dictate whether to be intimate with your spouse or not. Many times, we must act in faith before our feelings ever catch up with us. So just give it a shot and try to be intimate with your spouse at least once a week. You may just find that you will begin to enjoy it!

I have found that the deeper and more intimate my relationship with Christ has become, the deeper and more intimate I have become with my husband. Our marriages are truly a reflection of our relationship with our Savior. As I keep growing in intimacy with the Lord, the intimacy in my marriage keeps getting better and better.

Our whole Christian life is a pursuit to know Jesus more and to become more like Him, being transformed into His image. Many people know about Jesus, but they do not truly know Him. They may have grown up in church or know about Him through God's Word but have never encountered Him. When we spend time with Him in His presence through worship, prayer, and reading the Word of God, we will become more intimate with Him. God wants us to draw near to Him, and He will draw near to us (James 4:8). We are the ones who determine the level of our intimacy with the Lord. As you grow closer to Him, you will grow closer to your spouse.

Summary

- Sex is God's gift to marriage.
- The lack of intimacy in a marriage can have profound effects on the emotional and physical well-being of both partners and may even lead to the breakdown of their marriage.
- Intimacy is an essential part of any marriage. It provides a sense of security, love, and acceptance that is critical for a man's and woman's being.
- When we meet the sexual needs of our spouse, it not only benefits them, but it also helps to safeguard our marriage from sexual immorality. Just like the verse says in 1 Corinthians 7:2–5, we should not deprive each other of sexual relations.

- In sex, as with every relationship, nothing should be done out of selfish motivation but primarily to serve the interests of the other. In sex, the husband's goal should be his wife's pleasure, and the wife's goal should be her husband's pleasure.
- Our marriages are truly a reflection of our relationship with our Savior.
- We are the ones who determine the level of our intimacy with the Lord. As you grow closer to Him, you will grow closer to your spouse.

Questions

1. How is the Holy Spirit speaking to me through this chapter?

2. How is your level of intimacy with your spouse? Rate it on a scale of 1–10. Be honest.

3. How can you improve your level of intimacy with your spouse? What can you each do to better the intimacy in your marriage?

4. How is my intimacy with God? What can I do to deepen my intimacy with Him?

Prayer

Heavenly Father, I want to draw close to You, so You will draw close to me. I desire to be more intimate with You. I trust that as I grow closer to You, I will become closer to my spouse. I pray that You will help me to become more intimate in my marriage. Help us to meet each other's physical needs. I pray that our intimacy will be a blessing to both of us in Jesus's name. Amen.

CHAPTER 12

Financial Stewardship

He who is faithful in a very little thing is also faithful in much; and he who is dishonest in a very little thing is also dishonest in much. Therefore if you have not been faithful in the use of earthly wealth, who will entrust the true riches to you? And if you have not been faithful in the use of that [earthly wealth] which belongs to another [whether God or man, and of which you are a trustee], who will give you that which is your own? No servant can serve two masters; for either he will hate the one and love the other, or he will stand devotedly by the one and despise the other. You cannot serve both God and mammon [that is, your earthly possessions or anything else you trust in and rely on instead of God].

—Luke 16:10–13 (AMP)

Did you know that the Bible has more to say about finances than it does about faith, prayer, heaven, or hell? There are roughly 2,350 verses concerning money in the Bible. Jesus taught more on the subject of finances than on any other single topic. He taught more about managing resources than He did on prayer, or even faith, which tells us that the topic of money, and how we handle it, is very important. In Luke 16:11, Jesus tells us that if we cannot be faithful in our finances, then we cannot be trusted with anything.

Why am I talking about finances? Many couples quarrel about money. According to a survey by Ramsey Solutions, money fights are the second leading cause of divorce, behind infidelity. Results show that both high levels of debt and a lack of communication are major causes of the stress and anxiety surrounding household finances. When couples get married, they make a vow that says, "Till death do us part," but a more accurate vow for some marriages is "Till debt do us part."

You may not want to read a chapter on finances and how you should steward your money, but I am telling you that this chapter might just save your marriage. Sometimes the things you least want to hear about will help you the most. When we follow God's biblical principles for any area of our lives (whether that is for our marriage, finances, businesses, or relationships), we will be successful and experience the fruit that we want to see.

The very first thing that we need to understand about finances is we are stewards of what God has given us. A steward is a person who manages someone else's property, finances, or other affairs. As Christians, we are stewards, and we need to recognize that the money we have is not really ours. It is a gift from God. James 1:17 (NKJV) says, "Every good and perfect gift is from above." You may think that you are the one responsible for everything that you have earned. Ultimately, God is the source of everything and has allowed you the ability to have whatever it is that you have. Yes, you may have worked forty hours per week at your job, but God is the source. God gave you your life, your health, and abilities, and He is the One who opens the doors of opportunity. He is the source, and you are the steward who gets to manage it. "For we brought nothing into this world, and it is certain we can carry nothing out" (1 Timothy 6:7 NKJV).

Scripture makes it clear that our relationship with money and possessions is to be one of stewardship, not one of ownership. Once couples accept the fact that God owns everything and that they have simply been chosen to be stewards of His property, then it is important for them to manage according to His principles and standards. How we faithfully handle what He has given us will determine whether He will give us greater things to manage.

> The earth is the LORD's, and all its fullness, The world and those who dwell therein. For He has founded it upon the seas, and established it upon the waters. (Psalm 24:1–2 NKJV)

God gives us money because we need it to function in this world. We use it to buy the goods that meet our needs, but money is not what provides for us. The question is whether we are trusting in God as the source of our provision or whether we are operating out of fear and trusting in money itself. Money is just a delivery system; God is our source.

One of the ways that God can see whether or not we fully trust Him as our source is if we give tithes and offerings. God does not ask for tithes and offerings because He needs your money. He asks because He wants you to learn to trust Him with all your heart, and finances are the first step in that direction. The desire of God's heart is to be involved in every area of your life. He does not just want to be in your life for an hour at church or in your leftover time during the week. He wants all of you. The way God gets you to trust Him in the area of finances is by asking you to give a portion of what you earn back to Him, and He promises to bless you in return. You cannot outgive God.

Tithing is about giving our first to God. It is not about giving God what is left over after you've paid your bills. It always requires faith to give the first, which is why so few Christians actually experience the blessings of tithing. It does not take any faith to give the last. By tithing, you are saying, "God, I recognize You first. I am putting You first in my life, and I'm trusting You to take care of the rest of the things in my life." That is why tithing is so important. It is the primary way we acknowledge that God is first.

A tenth is what was tithed in the Old Testament. Since we are no longer under the law in the Old Testament and are living under the New Testament, do we still have to give a tenth of our earnings? Yes. The first tithe began with Abram about four hundred years before the Mosaic law. Since we are under the seed of Abraham, we tithe today to our High Priest Jesus, just as Abram did to Melchizedek. Because we are under the New Covenant, we should give above and beyond 10 percent because we have received so much more than those under the law, thanks to Jesus for his sacrifice and blood that was shed for us.

In 2 Corinthians 9:6–7, we are told that if we sow sparingly, then we will reap sparingly, and if we sow bountifully then we will reap bountifully. We are to give, not grudgingly or out of necessity, but from a cheerful heart. It is all about the heart. If we are giving only out of guilt or duty, then it is not going to be blessed. When we give out of a cheerful heart, then it will be blessed. I encourage you to give and tithe but do not do it out of fear or guilt. Do it because you love God and you want to show appreciation for all that He has done for you.

> Now (remember) this: He who sows sparingly will also reap sparingly, and he who sows generously (that blessings may come to others) will also reap generously (and be blessed). Let each one give (thoughtfully and with purpose) just as he has decided in his heart, not grudgingly or under compulsion; for God loves a cheerful giver (and delights in the one whose heart is in his gift). And God is able to make all grace (every favor and earthly blessing) come in abundance to you, so that you may always (under all circumstances, regardless of the need) have complete sufficiency in everything (being completely self-sufficient in Him), and have an abundance for every good work and act of charity. (2 Corinthians 9:6–8 AMP)

When you purify your motives for tithing and start doing it as you desire in your heart, I believe that you will begin to see a return on your giving, and you will probably want to start giving a lot more than 10 percent.

If money is going to be a source of oneness in marriage, you'll first need to realize that you are on a mission together. You are on the same team. Your mission is to steward God's resources, not simply accumulate wealth or live in comfort and ease. I have learned that in most relationships, there is one "spender" and one "saver." God made you different for a reason to balance each other out, so do not be critical of each other. Instead, work together to develop a plan. Unity is the key to making your finances work for you in your marriage.

> The plans of the diligent lead surely to abundance and advantage, but everyone who acts in haste comes surely to poverty. (Proverbs 21:5 AMP)

If you want to enjoy financial unity within your marriage, you will need to follow a game plan that you come up with together. First, address the financial problems that you have and then strategize to overcome them. Discuss what your goals are. Where are you right now, and where do you want to be with your finances? Create a written budget that works and stick to it. Communicate, communicate, communicate. When we avoid the topic of finances, it just buries the problem and creates more stress. The first step in getting help in any area of your life is to talk about it and bring everything to the surface. Putting a plan together will help reduce conflict about money in your marriage.

We must be good stewards of what God has given us. God has given each one of us time, talents, and treasures. One day we will stand before Him and be judged on what we did with what God gave us. Every single person will be tested in this area of finances. My husband and I finally got sick and tired of being sick and tired of our finances and decided to start doing things God's way. We started reading what the scriptures say about finances and applying them to our lives. I cannot say that we are where we want to be yet, but I can say that we thank God we are not where we used to be.

I remember one day when I was praying about our finances and the Lord spoke so clearly to my heart and said, "You cannot just pray your way out of debt. You must do something about it." He then related it to a person who is just praying to lose weight but does not take the steps necessary toward good health to achieve the desired weight loss. Financial success will not happen just by wishing for it or praying for it. It comes by working hard and implementing a plan to achieve your goals.

You will not see a change overnight but as you keep taking the steps necessary and working together, you will see a turnaround. Small changes eventually add up to yield huge results. Be faithful to steward well whatever God has given you so that He can trust you with more for His kingdom purposes.

Summary

- Jesus taught more on the subject of finances than on any other single topic.
- Many couples quarrel about money. According to a survey by Ramsey Solutions, money fights are the second leading cause of divorce, behind infidelity.
- When we follow God's biblical principles for any area of our lives (whether that is for our marriage, finances, businesses, or relationships), we will be successful and experience the fruit that we want to see.
- The very first thing that we need to understand about finances is that we are stewards of what God has given us.
- One of the ways that God can see whether or not we truly trust Him as our source is if we give tithes and offerings.
- If you and your spouse want to enjoy financial unity within your marriage, you will need to follow a game plan that you come up with together.
- Financial success will not happen just by wishing for it or praying for it. It comes by working hard and implementing a plan to achieve your goals.

Questions

1. How is the Holy Spirit speaking to me through this chapter?

2. Are we, as a couple, following God's principles regarding money? What do we need to *stop* doing, and what do we need to *start* doing?

3. Are my spouse and I being good stewards of what God has given to us? Are we putting Him first by giving Him the tithe (the first 10 percent of our income)?

4. What steps do we need to take to better steward our finances?

Prayer

God, thank You for giving Your Son for me. Thank You for Your sacrifice so I could be redeemed. I want to put You first in all areas of my life. Help me and my spouse honor You with the first fruits of our finances. We desire to be good stewards of what You have given us. Help us to be faithful with the little we have so You can trust us with whatever You want to give us in Jesus's name. Amen.

CHAPTER 13

Taking Care of You

Do you not know that your body is a temple of the Holy Spirit who is within you, whom you have [received as a gift] from God, and that you are not your own [property]? You were bought with a price [you were actually purchased with the precious blood of Jesus and made His own]. So then, honor and glorify God with your body.

1 Corinthians 6:19–20 (AMP)

I have been a personal trainer and group fitness instructor now for the past twenty-two years, and I am passionate about helping people get healthy from the inside out. This means being healthy not just physically but also mentally, spiritually, and relationally. For the first ten years of my personal training career, all I did was train the physical body of individuals. Then, as I grew in my relationship with God, I learned that we are a three-part being. We are a spirit who have a soul and live in a body. If we train only one and neglect the other two, then we are not going to be balanced. It all works together. In fact, I learned that as I focused more on training the inside (spirit and soul), the results came on the outside (body). The body is connected to the spirit. When we suffer mentally and spiritually, it will affect us physically. Whatever is going on inside of the body will manifest on the outside. As you get healthy on the inside, then you will also get healthy on the outside.

Again, this may be a chapter that you do not want to read but *need* to read. If we do not take care of ourselves, then how can we possibly take care of others? When you feel good yourself, you can then have the positive energy to share and take care of others. When we are healthy ourselves, it helps us to have healthy relationships with others as well. Being healthy is not about having a perfect body—it is all about feeling your best, not about how you look.

As husbands and wives, we tend to put everyone else's needs above our own. What happens is we end up tired, burned out, stressed, and miserable? When we are running around stressed out, our bodies will release a hormone called cortisol. While cortisol is an important hormone, too much can be a problem. When cortisol levels are constantly high, it can lead to weight gain, anxiety, depression, and other health problems. There are many ways to de-stress. Some things that I do daily include spending time with Jesus first thing in the morning, reading the Word of God, worshipping, praying, and just resting in God's presence. I also exercise, journal, play worship music throughout the day, go for walks with the family, and live with an attitude of gratitude. We must learn to "take" the time for ourselves each day and care for the temple that God has given us.

Being unhealthy will affect your marriage. It will affect how you are as a spouse, a parent, and a person. There is no such thing as fat and happy. People may say that to make themselves feel better, but being unhealthy does not make you happy—it makes you miserable. Good health is what feels good! I know the times that I was not taking care of myself were the times when I was the most miserable. On the other hand, when I exercise, eat healthy, get my mind right, feed my spirit with God's Word, listen to worship music, praise, and pray, then that is when I feel my best and can be the person that I want to be.

We have been given one body by God while we live here on earth. How are you going to steward it? God has given each of us 1,440 minutes each day. We cannot make the excuse that we do not have time, because we make time for whatever is important to us.

A one-hour workout is just 10% of your day. You may wonder how you can squeeze one hour of exercise into your day. You can do so by getting up early to exercise before work or by exercising at noon, in the evening after work, or by splitting it up throughout the day. Even thirty minutes of movement each day is effective and will burn calories, release positive endorphins, and make you feel better. Regular physical activity is one of the most important things you can do for your health. There are so many benefits to exercising. Research shows that regular workouts can boost your mood; increase your energy; help with weight loss; decrease feelings of depression, anxiety, and stress; strengthen your muscles and bones; improve your cardiovascular system; reduce your risk of chronic disease; delay skin aging; improve brain function and memory; help you sleep better; reduce pain; and improve your sex life. Exercise offers incredible benefits that can improve nearly every aspect of your health.

You may strongly dislike exercise, but I want to encourage you to do it anyway. After you have created a habit of exercising, your body will begin to "crave" it, and soon you will find yourself loving it and not wanting to miss a day of being active. I always tell people to find something that they enjoy doing, and they will most likely stick with it. Whether it is walking, biking, rowing, swimming, running, spinning, weightlifting, aerobic, or fitness classes—just find some activity that you enjoy doing and stay with it. Whatever you do consistently is what your body will crave. If you sit on the couch as a couch potato, do not expect your body to crave going on a run. On the other hand, if you consistently exercise, your body will eventually crave being active and will want to do more of it.

You may be saying, "Well, I just don't have the energy to exercise."

Let me tell you what I tell all my clients: It takes energy to create energy. Once you get moving, your body will release the positive hormones that will help you to have more energy and feel so much better. Just remember that your body is capable; it is your mind that you must convince. The hardest part is the beginning. Once you take the step to begin to exercise, you have won half the battle! Just keep moving forward one step at a time.

It is good to change your routine to keep your body from becoming complacent. Our bodies adapt so quickly that we need to keep shocking them with different activities to keep seeing results. I know so many people who do the same workout for the same length of time every single day. While it is good to still be exercising, your body will plateau, and you will not keep seeing positive results like you most likely want to see. Mix it up and do different things each day to keep the body guessing and seeing results!

I like to encourage people to set short-term goals. Sometimes when we set a big, long-term goal, it seems so unrealistic and unattainable. For instance, if you need to lose one hundred pounds, it can seem so daunting when all you think about is losing that much weight. However, when you set smaller, short-term goals, it makes them more attainable. If your long-term goal is to lose one hundred pounds, then set a short-term goal to lose seven pounds for the month. A healthy way to lose weight is one to two pounds per week. If you were to lose seven pounds per month, you would be down eighty-four pounds in one year and almost to your goal weight. When we reach those short-term goals each month, it motivates us to keep working and taking those healthy steps that we need to take to reach our long-term goals.

I love exercise and have a passion for it, but I know that we can exercise all we want, and if we do not change our eating habits, then we will not see any results. The saying, "You can't outrun your fork" is true. You can exercise all day long, but if you are not following it up with healthy eating, then you will not see the results that you want to see. Start by making small changes to your diet. Cut out soda or high-calorie drinks, sugar, and processed food. Just by doing this, you will see results. Drink more water. I recommend drinking at least eight 8-ounce glasses of water each day, and more if you exercise. Drink a glass of water before your meals. It will make you feel fuller, and you will not eat as much. Eat five small meals per day with some type of protein included with each meal.

Begin your day with a healthy breakfast. Just like you cannot start your car on an empty tank of gas, you cannot lose weight without fueling your body each day. Eat a healthy snack between breakfast and lunch. Have a good lunch, then another small snack between lunch and supper. Supper should be no later than two to three hours before bedtime, and it should be your lightest meal since you will not be burning off the calories before bedtime. I like to stick with just a protein and veggies for supper. Be sure to eat lean proteins, complex carbohydrates, healthy fats, fruits, and vegetables. Your body will thank you for it! Whatever food you eat, your body will crave. Stop eating all the junk food and start fueling your body with good, nutrient-rich foods, and your body will begin to crave them.

I have found that many women are emotional eaters, and are even addicted to food. We tend to eat when we are stressed, happy, depressed, bored, and everything in between. When you want to eat but you are not even hungry, ask yourself *why* you are eating. Are you stressed? Are you tired? Are you emotional? Are you bored? If you answered yes to any of those questions, it is best to occupy yourself by doing something productive and removing yourself from the situation. Also, pray and ask the Lord to give you self-control anytime you want to eat but do not need to be eating. God is faithful to help us when we ask for His help. I encourage you to pray for self-control before every meal, so you eat only what your body needs. Eat to live, do not live to eat.

One of the best ways to begin your transition to being healthy is by getting your mind right each day. Did you know that your attitude for the day is usually made up within the first ten minutes of waking? What you do for the first ten minutes of each day truly matters. My days always begin with coffee and Jesus. I begin by thanking the Lord for waking me up for the day and giving Him praise and thanks for all that I have. I also begin my days by reading the Word of God to renew my mind.

> Therefore I urge you, brothers and sisters, by the mercies of God, to present your bodies [dedicating all of yourselves, set apart] as a living sacrifice, holy and well-pleasing to God, which is your rational (logical, intelligent) act of

worship. And do not be conformed to this world [any longer with its superficial values and customs], but be transformed and progressively changed [as you mature spiritually] by the renewing of your mind [focusing on godly values and ethical attitudes], so that you may prove [for yourselves] what the will of God is, that which is good and acceptable and perfect [in His plan and purpose for you]. (Romans 12:1–2 AMP)

The only way to renew our minds is with God's Word. The Word of God is living and active. It is powerful, and it is the only thing that can transform our minds. When we read God's Word, we do not read it—instead, the Word reads us. The Bible is the only book that will judge the thoughts and attitudes of our hearts. When we read it, we become transformed and can have the mind of Christ (see 1 Corinthians 2:16).

For the word of God is living and active and full of power [making it operative, energizing, and effective]. It is sharper than any two-edged sword, penetrating as far as the division of the soul and spirit [the completeness of a person], and of both joints and marrow [the deepest parts of our nature], exposing and judging the very thoughts and intentions of the heart. (Hebrews 4:12 AMP)

The best way to begin your day is by reading the Word of God and having prayer time. It truly is amazing how God will speak to you when you open your Bible. He speaks through His living Word and will give you exactly what you need for each day. God's Word is a lamp unto our feet and a light unto our path (Psalm 119:105).

We must also take captive every negative thought (see 2 Corinthians 10:5) and think about those things that are true, honorable, pure, wholesome, lovely, and bring us peace (see Philippians 4:8). The mind truly is the battlefield. We can choose to dwell on negative thoughts or turn them around and focus on the Word of God. If you want your life to change in a positive direction, then you must implant the Word of God into your heart and mind. There is a quote by Lao Tzu that says, "Watch your thoughts, they become your words; Watch your words, they become your actions; Watch your actions, they become your habits; Watch your habits, they become your character; Watch your character, it becomes your destiny." When you think on God's Word and live by it, doing what it says, I guarantee that you will see the fruit in your life. God's Word does not return void (see Isaiah 55:11).

> We are destroying sophisticated arguments and every exalted and proud thing that sets itself up against the [true] knowledge of God, and we are taking every thought and purpose captive to the obedience of Christ. (2 Corinthians 10:5 AMP)

> Finally, believers, whatever is true, whatever is honorable and worthy of respect, whatever is right and confirmed by God's word, whatever is pure and wholesome, whatever is lovely and brings peace, whatever is admirable and of good repute; if there is any excellence, if there is anything worthy of praise, think continually on these things [center your mind on them, and implant them in your heart]. (Philippians 4:8 AMP)

> So will My word be which goes out of My mouth; It will not return to Me void (useless, without result), without accomplishing what I desire, and without succeeding in the matter for which I sent it. (Isaiah 55:11 AMP)

Not only does the Word of God renew our minds, but it also feeds our spirit. The Word, which is Jesus, is living water that refreshes and fuels our inner self. When I think of someone who does not read the living Word of God, I get a picture of a dry, desert land that is all cracked and parched, ready for a drink of water. That is how our spirit gets when we go without the One who created us. We dry up and cannot seem to figure out why we feel empty, weak, and stagnant. When Jesus met with the Samaritan woman at the well (see John 4:1–42 NIV), He told her, "Everyone who drinks this water will be thirsty again, but whoever drinks the water I give them will never thirst. Indeed, the water I give them will become in them a spring of water welling up to eternal life."

Jesus himself is the very Word of God. He calls himself the "bread of life," promising that whoever comes to Him will never hunger or thirst. When we come before Him and fill ourselves with God's Word, we can receive his salvation and be truly fulfilled. In John 6, after feeding five thousand men, plus women and children, Jesus speaks to the crowd again, this time offering them a different kind of bread, one that would never rot and would always keep people full. When the people asked for this bread, the Bible records, "Jesus said to them, 'I am the bread of life;' whoever comes to me shall not hunger and whoever believes in me shall never thirst" (John 6:35 ESV).

The only way to fulfill that longing inside of you is to fill yourself with Jesus. The more time that you spend with Him, the more you are conformed to His image. The only way that you will be the person that God created you to be and the person that you want to be is by spending time with Jesus.

> For physical training is of some value, but godliness (spiritual training) is of value in everything and in every way, since it holds promise for the present life and for the life to come. (1 Timothy 4:8 AMP)

I encourage you to take time for yourselves each day by spending time with Jesus, renewing your mind with the Word of God, exercising, and fueling your body with good, wholesome food. As you take care of yourself, you will then be able to better care for those people around you and be the spouse that you desire to be. The best way to get healthy is by doing it together with your spouse. When we have accountability, it will help us to stay on track and keep doing the things that we need to do. You need to be healthy to fulfill the plans that God has for you. So do not wait until Monday. Start today and take the steps needed toward a healthier *you*!

Summary

- Being unhealthy will affect your marriage. It will affect how you are as a spouse, a parent, and a person.
- Regular physical activity is one of the most important things you can do for your health.
- You can exercise all day long, but if you are not following it up with healthy eating, then you will not see the results that you want to see.
- One of the best ways to begin to be healthy is by getting your mind right each day.
- The only way to renew our minds is with God's Word. The Word of God is living and active. It is powerful, and it is the only thing that can transform our minds.
- The only way to fulfill that longing inside of you is to fill yourself with Jesus. The more time that you spend with Him, the more that you are conformed to His image. The only way that you will be the person that God created you to be and the person that you want to be is by spending time with Jesus.
- You need to be healthy to fulfill the plans that God has for you.

Questions

1. How is the Holy Spirit speaking to me through this chapter?

2. Am I taking care of the temple that God has given me? Would I consider myself healthy in body, mind, and spirit? Rate yourself on a scale of 1–10 in each area. How can you improve?

3. What changes do I need to make to become healthier? What changes do we need to make together as a couple?

4. What are some realistic goals (short- and long-term) that we can each set to become healthy? In what ways can we hold each other accountable?

Prayer

God, thank You for this body that You have given me. Forgive me when I have not cared for the temple that You have entrusted to me. Help me to take care of myself so I can do everything that You call me to do and bring honor and glory to Your name. I pray that my spouse and I can be healthy together. Show us what we need to do to become healthier in body, mind, and spirit in Jesus's name. Amen.

CHAPTER 14

Rejection

Although my father and my mother have abandoned me,
yet the LORD will take me up [adopt me as His child].
—Psalm 27:10 (AMP)

We've all experienced rejection. It may have been from a parent, a friend, a boyfriend/girlfriend, siblings, another member of the family, a spouse, or those who are closest to you. Rejection is a part of life, and everyone will experience it at some time or another. My husband and I both struggled with rejection from our childhood and brought it with us into our marriage. It was a major cause of conflict in our marriage as we were constantly rejecting each other for fear of being rejected.

Rejection can be defined as the sense of being unwanted. You desire people to love you, yet you believe that they do not. You want to be a part of a group, but you feel excluded. Somehow you are always on the outside looking in.

There are many different situations that can cause rejection. Many people experience rejection from a parent(s) if they feel that they were not wanted, never good enough, or were abused physically, emotionally, or sexually. They can also feel rejection from parents who were absent if they were given up for adoption, if their parents went through a divorce, or if their siblings disowned them. When kids are mistreated or bullied in school by their peers or friends, they can struggle with rejection. Betrayal, abuse, persecution, and exclusion can all lead to rejection. Let's face it: we have all been rejected at one time or another in our lifetime.

Jesus understood what it felt like to be rejected because He was rejected too. Jesus was rejected by those in His hometown. Even his own brothers rejected Him. The Romans rejected Him, the Jews despised Him, and when He was on the cross taking on the sins of the world, His own Father turned His face away. While Jesus was hanging on that cross, He said, "My God, My God, why have you forsaken Me?" (Matthew 27:46 NKJV). Jesus became sin, went through rejection, suffered, and was beaten, wounded, and bruised to deliver us from rejection.

> He is despised and rejected by men, a Man of sorrows and acquainted with grief. And we hid, as it were, our faces from Him; He was despised, and we did not esteem Him. Surely He has borne our grief and carried our sorrows; yet we esteemed Him stricken, smitten by God, and afflicted. But He was wounded for our transgressions, He was bruised for our iniquities; the chastisement for our peace was upon Him, and by His stripes we are healed. All we

like sheep have gone astray; we have turned, everyone, to his own way; and the LORD has laid on Him the iniquity of us all. (Isaiah 53:3–6 NKJV)

Rejection is a major stronghold, and acceptance in Christ is the central aspect of deliverance and salvation. Because of Christ's rejection, we can be accepted in the Beloved. We can be accepted through the blood of Jesus. We can be accepted by grace. We do not have to be perfect through legalism or keeping laws. We can be accepted by grace through faith.

When we are rejected, mocked, excluded, alienated, abused, neglected, abandoned, or not accepted, we must not give the devil a foothold by allowing him to harden our hearts through hate. We must not pull back and tuck away our hearts to protect ourselves from rejection. That is just self-preservation, and it only means that we aren't trusting in God to protect us so therefore, we think we must protect ourselves.

In those painful moments when we have been hurt, rejection tells us to shut down, put up walls, and isolate ourselves from everyone. When we isolate ourselves, it will then lead to loneliness. Loneliness leads to misery, and miserable people make others miserable. Misery and loneliness frequently lead to self-pity, where we are always feeling sorry for ourselves. Self-pity is just pride because it is all about us. The step following self-pity is often depression—moods of gloominess that settle over you. Depression is a branch from the root of rejection. Depression will then likely lead to something even more serious, which is despair and hopelessness. Despair can lead to death or suicide.

Rejection can also put you on a different path, which leads to a hardening of the heart. The hardness leads to indifference where you say that you do not care. You put up walls to try to protect yourself. After indifference comes rebellion. "Well, they're against me, so I'll be against them." This hardening of the heart can cause hate and bitterness, which defiles not only you but also many others (see Hebrews 12:15).

Many people hold God at arm's length because they have been hurt by others. They fear that God will reject them because of their weaknesses, just like people have. But God loves you no matter what and will never leave you or forsake you (Hebrews 13:6).

For many years of our own marriage, it seemed that we held each other at arm's length. There was a wedge between us. We would both take everything that was said so offensively. Offended people offend others. I personally had rejection wounds from my father, who was absent during my childhood, which ran deep. It was not until I got healed from those wounds and received love from my Heavenly Father that I was able to fully open myself up to my husband. I could then give him the love that he needed and receive the love that I needed. It also solved so many arguments when we would recognize what was in operation and why we were defensive with each other. We could see the root of the problem at hand and deal with it. People often do not realize how rejection from their childhood influences their relationships today. We must take those hurts to Jesus and allow Him to heal us so that we can have the healthy relationships that we desire.

Nobody likes to be rejected, but once you realize Christ's love for you and receive His acceptance, you know that no matter who rejects you, you are still loved by God. If people reject Jesus, then they will reject you.

> He came to that which was His own [that which belonged to Him—His world, His creation, His possession], and those who were His own [people—the Jewish nation] did not receive and welcome Him. (John 1:11 AMP)

Even when Jesus was rejected by His own, He did not just sit around in self-pity. He moved on to where people gladly received Him. And He told His disciples, "Whoever will not receive you nor hear your words, when you depart from that house or city, shake off the dust from your feet" (Matthew 10:14 NKJV). Jesus did not stay where He was tolerated; He went to where He was celebrated. He went to where people recognized and received His person, His purpose, and His power. He had God's full acceptance; therefore, He did not fear man's rejection. You have God's full acceptance too. To overcome rejection, you must always keep God's opinion of you in your mind. It does not matter what others think and say of you; it matters what God thinks and says of you.

Rejection experiences can leave us with deep wounds, whether we are aware of them or not. The good news is that God can heal you from the wounds that come from rejection, help you to accept yourself, and enable you to show His love to others.

The first step to overcoming rejection is to recognize the problem. Once you recognize it, you can deal with it. The second step is to forgive those who have rejected you. Forgiveness is not an emotion; it is a decision. Do not say, "I can't forgive" because in actuality, you are saying, "I won't forgive." Your fleshly nature may not be able to forgive, but you can choose to forgive by asking God to work His forgiveness in and through you. Next, make a decision to deal with the sour fruits that rejection has produced in your life, such as bitterness, resentment, hatred, and rebellion. Then, receive and believe what God has already done for you. "He made us accepted in the Beloved" (Ephesians 1:6 NKJV). Receive the spirit of adoption. Every day, say aloud that you reject the spirit of rejection and receive the spirit of adoption!

I remember when I was walking out my freedom in this area of my life, I had just met with a Christian counselor who was walking me through forgiveness and healing from rejection. Immediately afterward, I went to the grocery store, and the first three people that I ran into had rejected me at some time in my life. I felt so defeated and just wanted to put my head down as I was reminded of the painful times when those people rejected me. Then the Lord spoke clearly to me and told me to pick my head up, look the person in the eye, and talk to them. He revealed to me that the enemy was trying to keep me down in this place of feeling rejected, but God wanted me to walk in freedom. Something rose in me, and I was able to look that person in the eye and say hello with a smile on my face. I then declared that I was an overcomer and that Satan would not keep me pushed down in this pit of rejection any longer. "If God be for me, then who can be against me." Breakthrough happened for me that day.

Now I can look in the eye anyone who has betrayed or wronged me and know that it does not matter if they rejected me because my God loves me and is for me. I do not allow the enemy to win by trying to push me down with people rejecting me. I know that I will not always be able to please everyone, and that is OK. If I am pleasing God and have His approval, that is all that really matters.

> Am I now trying to win the favor and approval of men, or
> of God? Or am I seeking to please someone? If I were still

trying to be popular with men, I would not be a bond-servant of Christ. (Galatians 1:10 AMP)

Prayer is a very powerful weapon in the fight against rejection. Prayer brings you into the presence of God. Prayer opens your spirit to hear the truth of your acceptance through Christ. You also need to exercise the authority that Christ gave to you against the enemy. Jesus said, "Behold, I give you the authority to trample on serpents and scorpions, and over all the power of the enemy, and nothing shall by any means hurt you" (Luke 10:19 NKJV). We must exercise our authority when the enemy tries to come against us. Some of the ways that we do that are through prayer, through commands, and through decrees that we release through our words. It is important to exercise your authority over the enemy on a consistent basis.

When you are feeling the wounds of rejection spring up, here is a prayer to pray:

God, I thank You that I am loved by You. I thank you that I am accepted in the Beloved. I thank You that if You are for me, then who can be against me? I thank You that when I submit to You, I can resist the devil and he must flee in Jesus's name. I stand against any scheme of the enemy to bring rejection against me. I declare that no weapon formed against me shall prosper, and every tongue that rises against me in judgment, You shall condemn. I choose to forgive those who have wronged or rejected me. I surrender these hurts to You, God, and ask for You to heal my heart. Thank You for loving me, and helping me to walk in love toward others in Jesus's name. Amen.

Summary

- Let's face it … we have all been rejected at one time or another in our lifetime.
- Jesus understood what it felt like to be rejected because He was rejected too.
- Because of Christ's rejection, we can be accepted in the Beloved. We can be accepted through the blood of Jesus. We can be accepted by grace.

- People often do not realize how rejection from their childhood influences their relationships today. We must take those hurts to Jesus and allow Him to heal us so that we can have the healthy relationships that we desire.
- Rejection experiences can leave us with deep wounds, whether we are aware of them or not. The good news is that God can heal you from the wounds that come from rejection, help you to accept yourself, and enable you to show His love to others.
- The first step to overcoming rejection is to recognize the problem. Once you recognize it, you can deal with it. The second step is to forgive those who have rejected you. Forgiveness is not an emotion—it is a decision.
- Prayer is a very powerful weapon in the fight against rejection.

Questions

1. How is the Holy Spirit speaking to me through this chapter?

2. Am I struggling with any root of rejection? Am I experiencing sour fruit such as bitterness, resentment, hatred, and rebellion?

3. From whom have I experienced rejection? Have I forgiven them?

4. Have I asked God to heal me from those wounds of rejection? Have I received His love and acceptance?

Prayer

Lord, thank You that my worth is found in You. Thank You that You love me even when others do not receive me. Thank You that I do not need to fear the rejection of others because I am loved and accepted by You. Thank You that You are always with me and will never leave me nor forsake me in Jesus's name. Amen.

CHAPTER 15

Can You Hear Me?

Understand this, my beloved brothers and sisters. Let everyone be quick to hear [be a careful, thoughtful listener], slow to speak [a speaker of carefully chosen words and], slow to anger [patient, reflective, forgiving]; for the [resentful, deep-seated] anger of man does not produce the righteousness of God [that standard of behavior which He requires from us].
—James 1:19–20 (AMP)

I am going to be honest: This chapter is a hard one. I mean, really, how do you communicate when men and women think so differently, and women are from Venus and men are from Mars, right? My husband and I always joke that men think "blue," and women think "pink." I wish the answer were simple and that I could give you a ten-step program that would solve all your communication problems in your marriage. I am not going to do that. Instead, we are going to look at what the Bible says about communication.

Communication is vital if you want a healthy relationship with anyone, whether it be your spouse, kids, family, friends, employees, coworkers, etc. We were made for relationships—a relationship with God and a relationship with others. The only way to have a good relationship is to have two-way communication. I know what you are thinking, ladies: *How can I communicate with a husband who has "selective hearing" and does not like to talk?* That is what prayer is for. The good news is that God does not have selective hearing, and He hears our requests. If your husband struggles with "selective hearing," then pray and ask the Lord to help him in this area.

The Bible has a lot to say about communication. Let's look at what some of the scriptures say. James 1:19–20 (AMP) says, "Let everyone be quick to hear (be a careful thoughtful listener), slow to speak (a speaker of carefully chosen words and), slow to anger (patient, reflective, forgiving); for the (resentful, deep-seated) anger of man does not produce the righteousness of God (that standard of behavior which He requires from us)."

Many of us need to memorize this scripture and post it where we can see it every day. In the world we live in today, most people do not listen, are quick to speak their minds, and are quick to become angry. From our earliest years, we have been trained to give information and express our point of view. We are so quick to speak that we often do not listen to what others are saying. The average human attention span is 8.25 seconds. It takes focused attention and selflessness to be a good listener. The Bible says that fools have no interest in understanding and only want to air their own opinions (Proverbs 18:2). Spouting off before listening to the facts is both shameful and foolish (Proverbs 18:13). I have found that when I do not listen to my husband, I end up reaping what I sow, and he ends up not listening to me. But when I focus, make eye contact with him, listen, and engage in the conversation, then I end up getting that back in return.

> A fool has no delight in understanding, but in expressing his own heart. (Proverbs 18:2 NKJV)

> He who answers a matter before he hears it, it is folly and shame to him. (Proverbs 18:13 NKJV)

Communication takes focus and effort. These days, most of us are so preoccupied with our phones, which distracts us from being present and having conversations with others. Some people are so focused on other people's lives on social media that they are missing out on their own lives. A friend told me a story of how she watched three teenage girls get on a Ferris wheel and the whole time they were distracted by being on their phones, probably viewing other people's lives on social media. She said how they may have been on the ride, but they missed the ride. Do not miss out on what is going on in your own life because you are so focused on other people's lives. Enjoy your own ride!

Many years ago, when our boys were young, our life was consumed by them. I put the boys before my spouse, and everything revolved around them. It was not until my husband, and I went on a spa date that my eyes were opened to what was happening in our marriage. We went to a spa, where we got to sit in a hot tub together before having our massages. When we got in the hot tub, I remember my husband sitting across from me rather than beside me, and we had this awkward moment of not even knowing what to say to each other, since our kids were not there. It was an "aha" moment that we needed to put each other before our kids and work on the communication in our marriage. Otherwise, when the kids were grown up and gone, we would not even have a relationship or know how to communicate. That day was a turning point in our marriage. Now we go to the spa and cannot sit close enough to each other. We talk and share our innermost desires and dreams with one another. Those are our favorite dates!

> Let the words of my mouth and the meditation of my heart be acceptable in Your sight, O LORD, my strength and my Redeemer. (Psalm 19:14 NKJV)

The way that we say something is more important than the words that we speak. Our tone often carries more weight than the actual words that are spoken. We can say, "I love you," but if the tone that we say it in does not sound loving, then it is not going to be received. If we speak words in a defensive or critical tone, then it will be received defensively or critically. Our tone, body language, and intent are so important as we communicate with others. In fact, researchers have long found that communication comes first from body language, followed by tone of voice, with the words we speak coming in last.

Most human communication is actually nonverbal. We pick up on so many cues just through facial expressions and body language alone. Your tone matters. Effective communication requires an understanding of your tone of voice and the ability to control it to help communicate not only your message but also your intent. Before you speak, imagine how the person you are talking to perceives you. Sometimes you might not realize that a certain *edge* to your voice can make people feel that they must be on the defensive. Simply, adapt to a gentler tone.

> A soft and gentle and thoughtful answer turns away wrath, but harsh and painful and careless words stir up anger. (Proverbs 15:1 AMP)

How you speak, and what you and your spouse say to each other, greatly impacts your emotions and the quality of your relationship. Couples who show appreciation for each other by saying "Please" and "Thank you" often have the happiest marriages. It is amazing what gratitude and positive words of encouragement will do for your marriage. A good verse to pray each day is Psalm 19:14 (NKJV), "Let the words of my mouth and the meditation of my heart be acceptable in your sight, O Lord, my strength and my redeemer." Our speech should be gracious and pleasant, seasoned with salt so that we will know how to answer one another (Colossians 4:6).

> Let your speech at all times be gracious and pleasant, seasoned with salt, so that you will know how to answer each one [who questions you]. (Colossians 4:6 AMP)

When you want someone else to see your point of view, remember that it is not all about you. In fact, listening is just as important as talking. So be sure not to talk over the other person or interrupt them. Give them space to talk and know when it is time for you to be quiet for a moment. Listening to someone lets them know that you are not just trying to push a certain opinion on them. It is also a sign that you care about how they feel and want to know what they are thinking. Proverbs 10:19 (AMP) says, "When there are many words, transgression and offense are unavoidable, but he who controls his lips and keeps thoughtful silence is wise."

> When there are many words, transgression and offense are unavoidable, but he who controls his lips and keeps thoughtful silence is wise. (Proverbs 10:19 AMP)

Something I pray nearly every day is for God to set a guard over my mouth and to keep watch over the door of my lips (Psalm 141:3). I do not want to speak negative, critical, judgmental words about or to others. I do not want to grieve the Holy Spirit by the words that I speak. I do not want to sow bad seeds and therefore reap them in the future.

> Do not be deceived, God is not mocked; for whatever a man sows, that he will also reap. For he who sows to his flesh will of the flesh reap corruption, but he who sows to the Spirit will of the Spirit reap everlasting life. (Galatians 6:7–8 NKJV)

Ephesians 4:29 (AMP) says, "Do not let unwholesome [foul, profane, worthless, vulgar] words ever come out of your mouth, but only such *speech* as is good for building up others, according to the need *and* the occasion, so that it will be a blessing to those who hear [you speak]." Are the words that you are speaking building up others or are they tearing them down? Are they a blessing to those who hear you speak? Proverbs 18:21 (AMP) says, "Death and life are in the power of the tongue and those who love it and indulge it will eat its fruit and bear the consequences of their words." If this scripture does not put a holy fear in you, then I do not know what will. We will reap the fruit of our words, whether positive or negative. So choose your words wisely. If you cannot say anything positive, then do not say anything at all.

> Death and life are in the power of the tongue, and those who love it and indulge it will eat its fruit and bear the consequences of their words. (Proverbs 18:21 AMP)

In 1 Thessalonians 5:11 (AMP), we are told, "Therefore encourage *and* comfort one another and build up one another, just as you are doing." We are to encourage, comfort, and build each other up with our words, not tear each other down. When we speak negatively to or about others, we are tearing down God's creation. We may think that we are getting away with our negative words, but eventually, they will catch up to us, and we will reap the consequences of them. Proverbs 16:24 (NLT) says, "Kind words are like honey, sweet to the soul and healthy for the body." Our kind words are sweet to the soul and are healthy for the body. Wow!

Have you ever heard of Dr. Emoto's famous rice experiment and what happened regarding positive and negative words? The basic premise of the experiment is this—the words we say and the thoughts we think have an energy that can physically manifest over time. In Dr. Emoto's original experiment, he found that the rice that he spoke kind words to remained mostly white, while the rice that he spoke negatively to turned moldy, providing physical evidence of the power of positivity. Positive words with good intentions behind them nurture and encourage growth. Negative words with negative emotions literally rot and destroy.

> There is one who speaks rashly like the thrusts of a sword, but the tongue of the wise brings healing. (Proverbs 12:18 AMP)

> Anxiety in a man's heart weighs it down, but a good (encouraging) word makes it glad. (Proverbs 12:25 AMP)

> A soothing tongue [speaking words that build up and encourage] is a tree of life, but a perverse tongue [speaking words that overwhelm and depress] crushes the spirit. (Proverbs 15:4 AMP)

If you want to have effective communication with your spouse, then start by assessing the words that you are speaking. No one wants to listen to a person who constantly speaks negatively, complains, or nags. If you want others to listen to you, then speak positive, encouraging, life-giving words that will be a blessing to those who listen to you. Become a good listener. Show your spouse that you truly care by listening, making eye contact, and engaging in the conversation. Think before you speak and remember that your tone means more than the words that you speak. If you are struggling in this area of communication with your spouse, then pray and ask God to help you. He is always waiting for us to call upon Him, and He will be there to help. I pray that God gives you wisdom on how to effectively communicate with your spouse.

Summary

- Communication is vital if you want a healthy relationship with anyone, whether it be your spouse, kids, family, friends, employees, coworkers, etc.
- We are so quick to speak that we often do not listen to what others are saying. The average human attention span is 8.25 seconds. It takes focused attention and selflessness to be a good listener.
- Some people are so focused on other people's lives on social media that they are missing out on their own lives.
- The way that we say something is more important than the words that we speak. Our tone often carries more weight than the actual words that are spoken.
- How you speak and what you and your spouse say to each other greatly impacts your emotions and the quality of your relationship.
- We will reap the fruit of our words, whether positive or negative. So choose your words wisely.
- Positive words with good intentions behind them nurture and encourage growth. Negative words with negative emotions literally rot and destroy.

Questions

1. How is the Holy Spirit speaking to me through this chapter?

2. On a scale of 1–10, how would you rate the communication between you and your spouse? In what ways could you improve it?

3. Do I need to listen or engage more, make eye contact, talk with a better tone, or speak more positively? What changes do I need God to help me make in this area of communicating with my spouse?

4. What words have I been speaking over my spouse and marriage? Am I reaping the fruit of my words (positive or negative)?

Prayer

God, I pray that You would help me to effectively communicate with my spouse. Help me to listen, to be attentive, and to respond with positive, encouraging words. Help us to understand each other and seek to grow in our relationship by communicating with each other in Jesus's name. Amen.

CHAPTER 16

Your Spouse Is Not Your Garbage Can

Do not let unwholesome [foul, profane, worthless, vulgar] words ever come out of your mouth, but only such speech as is good for building up others, according to the need and the occasion, so that it will be a blessing to those who hear [you speak]. And do not grieve the Holy Spirit of God [but seek to please Him], by whom you were sealed and marked [branded as God's own] for the day of redemption [the final deliverance from the consequences of sin]. Let all bitterness and wrath and anger and clamor [perpetual animosity, resentment, strife, fault-finding] and slander be put away from you, along with every kind of malice [all spitefulness, verbal abuse, malevolence]. Be kind and helpful to one another, tender-hearted [compassionate, understanding], forgiving one another [readily and freely], just as God in Christ also forgave you.

—Ephesians 4:29–32 (AMP)

Your spouse is supposed to be your confidant, your best friend, the one that you can talk to about anything. While we should be able to talk about everything and share with one another about our day, sometimes we can end up spewing out all the negative things onto our spouse. I remember when I was sharing some things with my spiritual mentor, and she said something that I will not ever forget. She said, "Your spouse is not your garbage can." Just because we may want to vent to someone does not give us permission to spew everything onto our spouse.

Have you ever been around someone who just constantly complains and talks negatively? It drains you. You never feel good, energized, and joyful after hearing someone spew negative things.

When you want to complain or vent to someone, take it to the Lord. He can handle it. If you read the Psalms, you will see that David was constantly spewing out his emotions and everything that was going on in his life to God. He poured out his heart before the Lord. God knows how we feel anyway, so take it to Him, where He can give you His perspective on what is going on, change your attitude, and give you encouragement through His Word. Whenever we want to complain in prayer, we should follow the patterns of the Psalms, which lead us past ourselves and back to God. Our complaints should always lead us back to fixing our eyes on God, giving Him thanks and praise.

Do not wait for your spouse to come home to vent everything to them. Yes, we are supposed to be able to talk with our spouse and share things, but if you are just using them to complain, that does not honor the Lord. Your spouse is not your garbage can. One thing that we, as a family, try to do every night at our dinner table is ask what our highs and lows were for the day. This gives everyone an opportunity to share about their day. We can then celebrate, praising God for the highs, and gain perspective from each other on how we can look at the lows, seeking to handle them in a godly way.

God's Word says in Philippians 2:14 to do everything without complaining or arguing. There is a difference between talking through a situation to find a solution and just complaining about it. I am a person who believes that if we have a complaint about a situation, then let's find a solution. If we do not have a solution, then let's go to God in prayer about it.

Do all things without complaining and disputing. (Philippians 2:14 NKJV)

In 1 Thessalonians 5:16–18 (NIV), we are told, "Rejoice always, pray continually, give thanks in all circumstances; for this is God's will for you in Christ Jesus." This verse does *not* tell us, "Grieve always, talk about your problems continually, and complain in all circumstances." I love the quote that says, "If you complain, you will remain." If you want your circumstances to change, complaining is not the answer. Rejoicing, praying, and giving thanks is the answer. In fact, the more you speak out of the flesh, the more of that you will see. If you want things to change, speak out what God is saying. Spend time in prayer to hear what He is saying about the situation and find scripture to speak out whenever your flesh wants to complain.

Our words are just an overflow of what is in our hearts. Luke 6:45 (NLT) says, "A good person produces good things from the treasury of a good heart, and an evil person produces evil things from the treasury of an evil heart. What you say flows from what is in your heart." This scripture reminds us that what is inside of us will eventually come out in our words and deeds. What we say is a product of what is already within us. If you find negative words flowing from your mouth, then take time to examine what is in your heart. Ask the Lord to search your heart and point out anything offensive to Him. Pray and ask God to pluck out anything from your heart that is not of Him.

> Search me [thoroughly], O God, and know my heart;
> test me and know my anxious thoughts; and see if there
> is any wicked or hurtful way in me, and lead me in the
> everlasting way. (Psalm 139:23–24 AMP)

When the Lord points out something in you, do not let it condemn you, but allow it to convict and change you. Ask Him to help you deal with whatever it is and to create in you a clean heart.

> Create in me a clean heart, O God, and renew a right and
> steadfast spirit within me. (Psalm 51:10 AMP)

Just as our hearts are a critical organ for keeping our bodies healthy and alive, our spiritual hearts are just as important for keeping our spirits healthy and bearing good fruit in our lives. If our hearts are filled with the love of God and His Word, then we will have the fruits of the spirit flowing out of us (love, joy, peace, patience, kindness, goodness, faithfulness, gentleness, and self-control — Galatians 5:22–23). On the other hand, if our hearts are filled with negative things like unforgiveness, judgment, anger, bitterness, pride, jealousy, and greed, then our words and actions will reflect these qualities. This is a great reminder of the importance of guarding our hearts because everything flows from the heart. Proverbs 4:23 (NIV) says, "Above all else, guard your heart, for everything you do flows from it." We should regularly examine our hearts and seek God's help in purifying them.

> Watch over your heart with all diligence, for from it flow
> the springs of life. (Proverbs 4:23 AMP)

When we fill our hearts with good things, our words and actions will naturally reflect this goodness. However, if we allow negative thoughts and emotions to fester in our hearts, they will eventually come out in our words and actions. I always tell my kids that "garbage in equals garbage out." It matters what we watch, what we listen to, who we hang around, and what the condition of our heart is. Whatever we allow into our mind and heart will affect us and come out, either positively or negatively. What we say and do has an impact on those around us. Our words and actions can either build up or tear down, and we can influence others in positive or negative ways. By being mindful of this, we can choose to speak and act in ways that bring life and hope to those around us. Let us guard our hearts, speak words of life, and seek to honor God in all that we say and do.

> Whatever you do [no matter what it is] in word or deed,
> do everything in the name of the Lord Jesus [and in
> dependence on Him], giving thanks to God the Father
> through Him. (Colossians 3:17 AMP)

Too often, people try to rely on their own willpower to change and clean up their own mouths. It does not work this way. James 3:8 (NLT) says, "But no one can tame the tongue. It is restless and evil, full of deadly poison." If we look only at the fruit and do not get to the root, then nothing will change. Willpower will take you only so far. You must always look within and ask yourself, *What is going on inside of me? What have my thoughts been like? What have I allowed to take root in my heart?*

It is easy to find the fruit of people's lives in what they say and do. We can learn a lot about someone's heart by simply listening to what is coming out of their mouth. The fruit will speak of what is going on inside. Jesus said that a tree is known by its fruit, and the same is true for our lives. Everything begins with a thought. If we allow unkind thoughts to fill our minds, they will produce negative fruit in our words and actions. But the more we fill our minds with God's Word and thoughts that are pure, lovely, admirable, and praiseworthy (see Philippians 4:8), the better fruit we will produce, and the better we will be able to treat others.

The words that come out of your mouth are an indication of what is in your heart. The fruit reflects the root. Trees bear good fruit when they are healthy. They are rooted in good ground with a source of plentiful nutrients. If they are not, then they will either not produce fruit or they will produce bad fruit. So what kind of fruit are you producing? Do you need to dig up some unwholesome roots in your heart?

> Either make the tree good and its fruit good, or else make the tree bad and its fruit bad; for a tree is known by its fruit. Brood of vipers! How can you, being evil, speak good things? For out of the abundance of the heart the mouth speaks. A good man out of the good treasure of his heart brings forth good things, and an evil man out of the evil treasure brings forth evil things. But I say to you that for every idle word men may speak, they will give account of it in the day of judgment. For by your words you will be justified, and by your words you will be condemned. (Matthew 12:33–37 NKJV)

According to Matthew 12:36–37, we will give an account for every idle word that we speak on the Day of Judgment. The words that we say will either acquit us or condemn us. This scripture should put a holy fear in us about the words that we speak to others. The next time that you are tempted to let garbage fly out of your mouth to your spouse or to anyone else, reflect on this scripture and go spend some time talking to God. After all, He is the One who can truly help us with every situation and give us wisdom on how to handle it. Fill your heart with God's Word. The more Word that you get in you, the more Word that will naturally flow out of you. God's Word will transform your heart and mind, your speech will change, and the fruit that you produce in your life will change too. If you want to bear good fruit, then get to the root.

Summary

- "Your spouse is not your garbage can." Just because we may want to vent to someone does not give us permission to spew everything onto our spouse.
- When you want to complain or vent to someone, take it to the Lord instead. He can handle it.
- God knows how we feel anyway, so take it to Him, where He can give you His perspective on what is going on, change your attitude, and give you encouragement through His Word.
- Whenever we want to complain in prayer, we should follow the patterns of the Psalms, which lead us past ourselves and back to God. Our complaints should always lead us back to fixing our eyes on God, giving Him thanks and praise.
- There is a difference between talking through a situation to find a solution and just complaining about it.
- Our words are just an overflow of what is in our hearts.
- Just as our hearts are a critical organ for keeping our bodies healthy and alive, our spiritual hearts are just as important for keeping our spirits healthy and bearing good fruit in our lives.

Questions

1. How is the Holy Spirit speaking to me through this chapter?

2. Have I been using my spouse as a "garbage can"? Do I vent everything to them, or do I go to the Lord first?

3. Have I just been complaining, or do I talk through the situations to find a solution?

4. Take inventory of what is in your heart. Ask the Lord to show you anything that He wants to deal with that is bearing negative words or fruit in your life. What did He reveal to you? What do you need to repent of?

Prayer

Father, help me to guard my heart and mind. I pray that You would search me and examine me. Point out anything that is offensive to You (Psalm 139:24). Create in me a clean heart and renew a steadfast spirit within me (Psalm 51:10). I pray that I will bring You all my emotions whenever I am tempted to complain to others. Help me to be a person who speaks life to others rather than speak words of death in Jesus's name. Amen.

CHAPTER 17

The Last Will Be First

It is not this way among you, but whoever wishes to become great among you shall be your servant, and whoever wishes to be first among you shall be your [willing and humble] slave; just as the Son of Man did not come to be served, but to serve, and to give His life as a ransom for many [paying the price to set them free from the penalty of sin].

—Matthew 20:26–28 (AMP)

Jesus set a great example for all of us in that He did not come to earth to be served, but to serve others. So often, we are so focused on me, myself, and I that we do not look around to see the needs of people that God has put in our lives. We were made to serve God and to serve others. I can guarantee you that when your focus is on yourself and on all that you can get, you will be a very miserable person. But the moment you start giving your time, talents, and treasures, you will find a joy that you never knew you could have. I love the acronym JOY, which stands for Jesus, Others, Yourself. When we keep serving Jesus first, then others second, and lastly ourselves, we will have JOY! Scripture tells us that is better to give than to receive (Acts 20:35). The amplified version of this verse even says that it is more blessed (and brings greater joy) to give than to receive.

> In everything I showed you [by example] that by working hard in this way you must help the weak and remember the words of the Lord Jesus, that He Himself said, "It is more blessed [and brings greater joy] to give than to receive." (Acts 20:35 AMP)

So often in our marriage, we think, *What can my spouse do for me?* Instead, we should be asking, *How can I better serve my spouse?* Have you ever asked your spouse the question of how you can better serve them? We are to serve one another in love. Galatians 5:13 (AMP) says, "For you, my brothers, were called to freedom; only do not let your freedom become an opportunity for the sinful nature (worldliness, selfishness), but through love serve and seek the best for one another."

Our flesh is selfish and thinks only about pleasing itself. As Christians, we are to become more and more like Jesus, but the only way to do that is by spending time with Him. We will become what we behold. When you are intimate with Him, you will have His heart, and you will naturally want to serve others. I know that whenever my focus is on myself, it is time for me to shift my eyes back on Jesus and spend time with the One who sacrificed Himself for all of us.

The Bible tells us to be devoted to one another in love and honor one another above ourselves (Romans 12:10). Another version says to outdo one another in showing honor. Honor is something that is missing in our culture. Many people have not been shown how to honor others. When we show honor to others in the way that we treat them, it pleases God. When we honor our leaders (whether we agree with them or not), it pleases God. When we honor those in authority over us (whether they treat us well or not), it pleases God. When we show honor to our spouse, it pleases God. Have you ever tried to outdo your spouse in showing honor? I challenge you to try it. When you honor others, it honors God, and you will receive honor in return.

> Be devoted to one another with [authentic] brotherly affection [as members of one family], give preference to one another in honor. (Romans 12:10 AMP)

> Be kindly affectionate to one another with brotherly love, in honor giving preference to one another. (Romans 12:10 NKJV)

We have all heard the saying, "You reap what you sow." It is true. Whatever seeds you plant is the harvest that you will reap. When we love others, God will send people on our path to love us. When we honor others, we will in turn be honored. When we are kind to others, people will be kind to us. When we give to others, it will be given back to us. Whatever you pour out is what you will get in return. The same is true if we sow hatred and dishonor—we will reap that which we have sown.

> Do not be deceived, God is not mocked [He will not allow Himself to be ridiculed, nor treated with contempt nor allow His precepts to be scornfully set aside]; for whatever a man sows, this and this only is what he will reap. For the one who sows to his flesh [his sinful capacity, his worldliness, his disgraceful impulses] will reap from the flesh ruin and destruction, but the one who sows to the Spirit will from the Spirit reap eternal life. Let us not grow weary or become discouraged in doing good, for at the proper time we will reap, if we do not give in. (Galatians 6:7–9 AMP)

The Bible tells us to give and it shall be given to us, but with a greater measure in return (Luke 6:38). Jesus was never thinking about himself. He was too busy serving others by healing the sick, raising the dead, or casting out demons. Everywhere He went, He helped people. Is that your heart's motive? That should be our motivation every day to look for opportunities to help and be a blessing to other people. There are opportunities to serve and to give to others around us every day. Have you taken the time to look around and see? What about your spouse? Have you even looked or asked God what they need for that day and how you can serve or give to them? Sometimes we are so busy serving others that we neglect our spouse the most. Why should they get the leftovers? It is a challenge every day to not be concerned with your own self but to be concerned with others instead. We must die to our selfish nature daily, just like the apostle Paul did (1 Corinthians 15:31).

> I affirm, by the boasting in you which I have in Christ Jesus our LORD, I die daily. (1 Corinthians 15:31 NKJV)

Whatever we give out is what we are going to receive in return. Read the Amplified and the Message versions of Luke 6:38 down below. It will make you want to be aware of what you are giving out to others.

> Give, and it will be given to you. They will pour into your lap a good measure—pressed down, shaken together, and running over [with no space left for more]. For with the standard of measurement you use [when you do good to others], it will be measured to you in return. (Luke 6:38 AMP)

> Don't pick on people, jump on their failures, criticize their faults—unless, of course, you want the same treatment. Don't condemn those who are down; that hardness can boomerang. Be easy on people; you'll find life a lot easier. Give away your life; you'll find life given back, but not merely given back—given back with bonus and blessing. Giving, not getting, is the way. Generosity begets generosity. (Luke 6:38 MSG)

I love the scripture verse in Proverbs 11:25 (NIV) that says, "A generous person will prosper; whoever refreshes others will be refreshed." Whenever we do good to others and refresh them, we have a promise that we will not only prosper but we will also be refreshed. God sees all that we do, whether good or bad. Nothing goes unnoticed by God. One of the names of God is El Roi, which means "the God who sees me." God sees all that you do for your spouse and for others. He sees the sacrifice, the giving, and all the things that happen behind the scenes. Even when nobody else sees, God sees. You will be rewarded for the good that you do when done with the right heart and motivation.

We should never be giving or serving out of duty or because we want to be noticed, and we shouldn't be serving just for a reward. The scripture says in Matthew 6:3 (NLT), "But when you give to someone in need, don't let your left hand know what your right hand is doing." Everything that we do is to be done unto the Lord (Colossians 3:23).

> Whatever you do [whatever your task may be], work from the soul [that is, put in your very best effort], as [something done] for the LORD and not for men, knowing [with all certainty] that it is from the LORD [not from men] that you will receive the inheritance which is your [greatest] reward. It is the Lord Christ whom you [actually] serve. (Colossians 3:23–24 AMP)

I believe that we will be judged according to how we serve God and others, especially in our own homes. Home is our first ministry. Harold B. Lee said, "The most important work that you will ever do is within the walls of your own home." If you cannot serve well in your own home, then you have no business serving and doing ministry elsewhere. It should begin first in the home and flow from that place. The Lord taught me a lot about serving in my home while raising kids. When you look at everything you do as an act of worship to God, it will change your perspective. You will not look at doing dishes, laundry, cleaning, and cooking dreadfully because you know that as you keep the right heart attitude, you can do all those things unto God. It is the Lord Jesus Christ whom you are serving.

I now view my times of cleaning, laundry, dishes, and cooking for my family as a time to worship and pray. It is amazing how fast time will go and how much more enjoyable it is when you get the right heart attitude and perspective. Also, when God sees that we can serve behind the scenes cheerfully and be faithful right where we are, then He can trust us with other things. After all, why would God give us any more if we complain about all that we already have?

God rewards faithfulness and is watching to see not just how we handle money, but how we steward everything we have been trusted with. If we cannot be trusted with the little, then God will not be able to trust us with the bigger things. If we cannot be trusted in our own homes to serve our spouse and children well, then don't plan on God entrusting you with anymore. It is being faithful to the little things that forge our character and prepare us to handle the big things. Your spouse and children are God's gift to you. Do not take them for granted.

> He who is faithful in what is least is faithful also in much; and he who is unjust in what is least is unjust also in much. Therefore, if you have not been faithful in the unrighteous mammon, who will commit to your trust the true riches? And if you have not been faithful in what is another man's, who will give you what is your own? (Luke 16:10–12 NKJV)

Every small act of service is an act of beautiful worship and praise when it is done for the Lord from a heart of love. It may often seem to us that our small contributions to the kingdom are insignificant, but when we are where God has called us to be (whether that is being a stay-at-home mom, a businessman or businesswoman, a leader, minister, teacher, doctor, nurse, construction worker, etc.), there is no act of service that is insignificant to the Lord. Each small act of love and service adds up to a life that is completely devoted to God and poured out for His glory.

God chose David after he learned lessons from being a shepherd boy among his father's sheep. The faithfulness he learned in that place prepared him to shepherd the inheritance of God—His people. God was able to trust David with this huge responsibility because of his faithfulness in the hidden place of the sheepfold. In these places where only God saw him, the Lord developed the right heart in David and the set of skills necessary for him to be the next king of Israel. The question is, will we be found faithful to God in the small, hidden, seemingly insignificant moments? If we can be faithful, then God can trust us with the purpose and destiny that He has for us!

I believe that someday when we get to heaven, we will be surprised to see the ones that God has rewarded the most. Many of them will be people you have never even heard about. They will be the humble ones, the ones behind the scenes, the no-names who put others before themselves and humbly served God and others in whatever ways that they could. Jesus tells us in Matthew 19:30 (AMP), "But many who are first (in this world) will be last (in the world to come); and the last, first."

> But many who are first [in this world] will be last [in the world to come]; and the last, first. (Matthew 19:30 AMP)

> So those who are last [in this world] shall be first [in the world to come], and those who are first, last. (Matthew 20:16 AMP)

There are so many ways that we can serve our spouse. You can make them coffee or breakfast, write a letter, pray for them, ask them what you can do to help them today, send them an encouraging text, buy them their favorite drink, take them on a lunch date, leave a note in their car or on the mirror, make their favorite dinner, affirm them, or just ask how you can better serve them. It truly is the little things in life that mean the most. Find out what their love language is and serve them in that way. If you have never read *The 5 Love Languages* by Gary Chapman, then I highly recommend that you read it with your spouse. According to Chapman, we all give and receive love in five different ways (words of affirmation, acts of service, receiving gifts, quality time, and physical touch). Find out how you and your spouse like to give and receive love. It is almost always different from each other, which is why we usually don't know how to speak one another's love language because we tend to give how we want to receive, completely unaware that our spouse receives love differently.

I encourage you to read his book and take the 5 Love Languages test with your spouse. Learn how to speak each other's love language. Gary's book helped our marriage so much! We studied it four or five different times and even led a Bible study on it. It was interesting to see that as we grew in our marriage, our love languages did change over time. Now, we have the same top two love languages. So I encourage you that even if you have taken the test with your spouse, redo it and see what you find. You might just be surprised!

How can you serve your spouse today? What can you do to show them honor? Remember, the seeds that you sow today will be what you reap in the future. What good seeds will you be planting?

Summary

- So often, we are so focused on me, myself, and I that we do not look around to see the needs of the people that God has put in our lives. We were made to serve God and to serve others.
- So often in our marriage, we think, *What can my spouse do for me?* Instead, we should be asking, *How can I better serve my spouse?*
- When you honor others, it honors God, and you will receive honor in return.
- Whatever you pour out is what you will get in return.
- Sometimes we are so busy serving others that we neglect our spouse the most. Why should they get the leftovers? It is a challenge every day to not be concerned with your own self and be concerned with others instead.
- I believe that we will be judged according to how we serve God and others, especially in our own homes. Home is our first ministry. Harold B. Lee said, "The most important work that you will ever do is within the walls of your own home."
- It is being faithful to the little things that forge our character and prepare us to handle the big things. Your spouse and your children are God's gift to you. Do not take them for granted.

Questions

1. How is the Holy Spirit speaking to me through this chapter?

2. Am I focused on what can be done for myself, or am I looking for ways to better serve my spouse? In what ways can I serve my spouse more? List ten ways.

3. What seeds have I sown that I am now reaping? Am I sowing positive or negative seeds into my marriage?

4. What is my spouse's love language? What is my love language? Are we speaking each other's love language? How could we each do a better job of speaking one another's love language?

Prayer

Heavenly Father, thank You for sending your Son, Jesus to be the perfect example of a servant. Please show me how to better serve You and others. Help me to remember to do everything as an act of worship unto You. I want to be found faithful in the little so that You can trust me with much. Help me to better serve my spouse and bring honor to You, in Jesus's name. Amen.

CHAPTER 18

Stop Pointing the Finger

Judge not that you be not judged. For with what judgment you judge, you will be judged; and with the measure you use, it will be measured back to you. And why do you look at the speck in your brother's eye, but do not consider the plank in your own eye? Or how can you say to your brother, 'Let me remove the speck from your eye'; and look, a plank is in your own eye? Hypocrite! First remove the plank from your own eye, and then you will see clearly to remove the speck from your brother's eye.

—Matthew 7:1–5 (NKJV)

Most people do not realize that many of the relationship issues we have in our lives are a result of our own judgment. When we judge others, we will be judged, and with the measure we use, it will be measured back to us. Whatever we sow is what we are going to reap in our own lives. People may think that they can get away with judging others, pointing the finger, criticizing, slandering, or gossiping but the truth is, we will reap exactly what we have sown. Whatever seeds we plant in one season are the harvest that we will receive in another season.

> Do not be deceived, God is not mocked; for whatever a man sows, that he will also reap. (Galatians 6:7 NKJV)

My mentor taught me that whenever my finger was pointed at my spouse, I needed to look at the other three fingers pointing back at myself. It is so easy for our prideful human nature to point the finger and try to put the blame on someone else, rather than doing a little introspection to see what's going on in our own hearts. The moment that we become aware of our own weaknesses and sins, we will be less likely to point out the weaknesses and sins of other people. God is the only Judge. Someday, He will settle every matter and pay back for whatever was done to us and what we have done to others. It is not our job to point the finger and judge. It is His. The only thing that we get when we judge others is judgment ourselves.

> Judge not, and you shall not be judged. Condemn not, and you shall not be condemned. Forgive, and you will be forgiven. Give, and it will be given to you: good measure, pressed down, shaken together, and running over will be put into your bosom. For with the same measure that you use, it will be measured back to you. (Luke 6:37–38 NKJV)

There is a law of harvest or sowing and reaping that implies both to the positive and the negative. If we sow good things, then we will reap good things in return. On the other hand, if we sow bad things, we will reap those things in return. If a farmer plants corn, he will get corn in return. You get exactly what you sow or plant. Actually, we reap more than what we sow. We can see in the verses above in Luke 6:37–38 that if we judge, we will be judged. Whatever we give out will be given back to us, a good measure—pressed down, shaken together, and running over. With the standard of measurement that we use, it will be measured back to us in return. When judgments go out from us, that is what is going to come back to us, but with good measure, pressed down and running over. If it seems as though you are constantly being judged, you might ask yourself if you have been judging others. It seems that we are always quick to judge or say something about someone else, but not so quick to look within and examine our own hearts.

Judging is about giving a final verdict on another person, like a judge would. It is not saying that they didn't do something or that something didn't happen. You are not denying what happened with that person. Judgment is passing a verdict on a person's character or motives. We can address the action, but it is not our job to pass judgment and put a label on a person. God is the only one to render judgment. When we are taking the place of a judge, then God will not be our judge in the situation. When we repent of the judgment and ask Him to forgive us, then God can go to work in the situation.

With the law of harvest, we reap later than when we sow. There is always a period of time between planting and reaping. A farmer does not go out and plant seeds one day and then expect his harvest to spring up the very next day. No, there is always a season between sowing and reaping. That is why when people sow to the flesh (see Galatians 5:16–17), because they don't immediately reap the consequences, they think that they got away with judging, cursing, slandering, gossiping, etc. Galatians 6:7 (NLT) tells us, "Do not be misled – you cannot mock the justice of God. You will always harvest what you plant." Don't think that you will get away with pointing the finger at others. You cannot violate the law of the harvest and get away with it. You will reap whatever you sow. That is why it is so important to understand these principles and abide by them. When you fall short, repent quickly and turn from those ways.

Walking in the Spirit

I say then: Walk in the Spirit, and you shall not fulfill the lust of the flesh. For the flesh lusts against the Spirit, and the Spirit against the flesh; and these are contrary to one another, so that you do not do the things that you wish. But if you are led by the Spirit, you are not under the law. Now the works of the flesh are evident, which are: adultery, fornication, uncleanness, lewdness, idolatry, sorcery, hatred, contentions, jealousies, outbursts of wrath, selfish ambitions, dissensions, heresies, envy, murders, drunkenness, revelries, and the like; of which I tell you beforehand, just as I also told you in time past, that those who practice such things will not inherit the kingdom of God. But the fruit of the Spirit is love, joy, peace, longsuffering, kindness, goodness, faithfulness, gentleness, self-control. Against such there is no law. And those who are Christ's have crucified the flesh with its passions and desires. If we live in the Spirit, let us also walk in the Spirit. Let us not become conceited, provoking one another, envying one another. (Galatians 5:16–26 NKJV)

It is so important to stay connected to God each day through prayer and by reading His Word. That is the only way that you can walk according to the Holy Spirit. Otherwise, we will want to gratify the desires of the flesh, which are always contrary to the Spirit. Galatians 5:16–17 (NIV) says, "So I say, walk by the Spirit, and you will not gratify the desires of the flesh. For the flesh desires what is contrary to the Spirit, and the Spirit what is contrary to the flesh. They are in conflict with each other, so that you are not to do whatever you want." To not respond according to our flesh, we must be connected to God and walk in the Spirit. Only then can we produce the fruit of the Spirit, which is love, joy, peace, patience, kindness, goodness, faithfulness, gentleness, and self-control (Galatians 5:22–23).

The judgments that we make and the words that we speak about others carry so much power. I have witnessed it in my own life. I remember early on in my marriage when my husband and I would have a fight, I would run to my mom and my sister to talk about it so they would take *my* side. I remember one night overhearing my husband do the same thing back to me by sharing some things with my brother. It hurt my heart so much to overhear him saying those things about me, but then I was quickly reminded that I had just done the same thing to him, and I was reaping what I had sown. I learned to stop speaking negatively about my husband to anyone, and that our problems were to stay between us unless we were sharing them with a counselor, pastor, or mentor to find solutions to the problems. We should never talk negatively about our spouse to our friends or family members unless we want to reap the consequences of that. It will only make matters worse. Learn how to talk through your problems with your spouse and not share them with everyone else.

> Death and life are in the power of the tongue, and those who love it and indulge it will eat its fruit and bear the consequences of their words. (Proverbs 18:21 AMP)

Our words carry so much power. Proverbs 18:21 (AMP) says, "Death and life are in the power of the tongue, and those who love it and indulge it will eat its fruit and bear the consequences of their words." Did you hear that? We will bear the consequences for our words. The negative words that you speak are what you will see. I remember a time when my husband and I kept saying to our girls, "You girls just don't listen," or "You never listen to us." It seemed that every time we spoke those words, we would get what we had said, and they would not listen. In fact, their listening only got worse. It finally occurred to me one day that we were reaping our negative words. We repented to God and to them for our judgments and negative words. We started speaking out and thanking God, saying, "Our girls do listen and obey us."

You know what happened … they started listening to us. Anytime we are saying always or never, we better check to see whether we have made a judgment and be quick to repent of it. When you find yourself saying, "He or she will never change" or "They will always be like that," then you have passed judgment and need to repent. When you pass judgment on someone else, you are giving an open door for the very same thing that you judged to occur in your own life.

We see all the time people who have passed judgment on their parents and then grow up to do the exact same thing that they judged their parents for. They may have had an alcoholic parent and judged them by saying, "I would never do that." Guess what, they end up becoming alcoholics and doing the very same thing that they despised. Or they judged their mom or dad saying, "I will never be like them or act like that." Then they wonder why they act exactly like them. I can look back at my life and see several times where I have made a judgment on someone and then ended up doing the exact same thing. If you can relate to this, think back to where you may have passed judgment and repent of it. Ask God to forgive you and release you from any judgments that you have made. Seeds sown that have not been dealt with in our lives will come back to us in ways that we never thought they would. The good news is you can repent and be freed from those judgments.

Do not curse your husband or children unless you want to reap that in return. Be a person who speaks blessing over others. James 3:9–10 (NLT) says, "Sometimes it praises our Lord and Father, and sometimes it curses those who have been made in the image of God. And so blessing and cursing come pouring out of the same mouth. Surely, my brothers and sisters, this is not right!" When blessing comes out of you, blessings will come back to you—good measure, pressed down, shaken together, running over, poured into your lap. Learn to confess and repent. You can be free from any judgments you have made that have been returned to you. The Bible says in 1 John 1:9 (NKJV), "If we confess our sins, He is faithful and just to forgive us *our* sins and to cleanse us from all unrighteousness." Jesus paid a high price for our sins. His mercy will cover us in a moment when we activate it with confession and repentance.

> But no one can tame the human tongue; it is a restless evil [undisciplined, unstable], full of deadly poison. With it we bless our Lord and Father, and with it we curse men, who have been made in the likeness of God. Out of the same mouth come both blessing and cursing. These things, my brothers, should not be this way [for we have a moral obligation to speak in a manner that reflects our fear of God and profound respect for His precepts]. (James 3:8–10 AMP)

I encourage you to sit down and spend some time with the Lord. Ask Him to bring to your mind any judgments that you have made against your spouse or anyone else. Make a list of people that you have made judgments against, even if they have been against yourself. Confess, repent, and ask God to cleanse you of those judgments. He will be faithful to forgive you of all your sins and cleanse you from all unrighteousness (1 John 1:9). Maybe you need to even go to your spouse or another person and confess your sins to them and ask for forgiveness. Do whatever the Lord is leading you to do and be quick to obey. When we confess our sins to one another and pray for one another, we can be healed and restored (James 5:16).

> Therefore, confess your sins to one another [your false steps, your offenses], and pray for one another, that you may be healed and restored. The heartfelt and persistent prayer of a righteous man (believer) can accomplish much [when put into action and made effective by God—it is dynamic and can have tremendous power]. (James 5:16 AMP)

I remember one time when the Lord was asking me to repent to my husband for something. I was being stubborn and disobedient. Then one night, God woke me up at 3:00 a.m. and I heard so clearly in my spirit the words, "James 4:17." I quickly got up and opened my Bible to see what it said. James 4:17 (AMP) says, "So any person who knows what is right to do but does not do it, to him it is sin." I knew that if I did not obey and repent like God was asking me to do, then I would be sinning against Him. I woke my husband and repented to him right away. His reply was, "OK, I love you and forgive you. Now let's go back to bed." I was so relieved to obey God and receive forgiveness. Why was it so hard for me to just humble myself and repent?

I have learned that delayed obedience is disobedience. When God tells you to do something, no matter how small it may seem, just be obedient. You never know what that one little act of obedience might do for you or for a relationship. Your obedience in one area may activate the breakthrough that you need in another area of your life. I have seen this before in my own life. One little act of obedience in one relationship opened the door for restoration in another relationship. Your follow-through is key to your breakthrough!

I pray that the next time that your finger wants to point at your spouse or anyone else in judgment, you look at the fingers pointing back at you and understand that you are going to reap whatever you sow. Let this put a holy fear in you to keep your heart free of judgment and to repent whenever you feel the Lord prompting you to repent.

Summary

- Whatever seeds we plant in one season are the harvest that we will receive in another season.
- The moment that we become aware of our own weaknesses and sins, we will be less likely to point out the weaknesses and sins of other people.
- To not respond according to our flesh, we must be connected to God and walk in the Spirit. Only then can we produce the fruit of the Spirit, which is love, joy, peace, patience, kindness, goodness, faithfulness, gentleness, and self-control (Galatians 5:22–23).
- Learn how to talk through your problems with your spouse and not share them with everyone else.
- Seeds sown that have not been dealt with in our lives will come back to us in ways that we never thought they would. The good news is, you can repent and be freed from those judgments.
- Confess, repent, and ask God to cleanse you of those judgments. He will be faithful to forgive you of all your sins and cleanse you from all unrighteousness (1 John 1:9).
- You never know what that one little act of obedience might do for you or for a relationship. Your obedience in one area may just activate the breakthrough that you need in another area of your life. Your follow-through is key to your breakthrough!

Questions

1. How is the Holy Spirit speaking to me through this chapter?

2. Examine your own heart: What judgments have I made on my spouse or on others? Is there anything that I need to repent of?

3. Am I reaping the words and judgments that I have been sowing? Am I experiencing the very thing that I judged someone else for?

4. Am I talking bad about my spouse to anyone else, or am I keeping our problems between the two of us (or a counselor, pastor, or mentor)? Am I reaping the consequences of my own words?

Prayer

Father, forgive me for any judgments that I have made against my spouse or anyone else. I lay down my self-imposed responsibility to judge the heart, motives, intentions, and actions of people. I repent of my pride when I am critical or have judgmental thoughts. Forgive me for any thoughts or words that I have made or spoken against others. Cleanse my heart and remove any bitter roots that would cause me to judge others, in Jesus's name. Amen.

CHAPTER 19

The Power of Unity and Agreement

Again I say to you, that if two believers on earth agree [that is, are of one mind, in harmony] about anything that they ask [within the will of God], it will be done for them by My Father in heaven. For where two or three are gathered in My name [meeting together as My followers], I am there among them.

—Matthew 18:19–20 (AMP)

If we truly understood the power of these scriptures in Matthew 18:19–20, I think we would make it a priority to walk in harmony and be in agreement with one another. These scriptures say that if two believers on earth agree (are of one mind, in harmony) about anything that they ask (within the will of God), it will be done for them by our Father in heaven. There is power in our agreement. The enemy knows the power we would have if we walked in unity and stood in agreement with each other in prayer. Unity is where the Spirit dwells. That is the place where the Lord releases His blessings.

> Behold, how good and how pleasant it is for brothers to dwell together in unity! It is like the precious oil [of consecration] poured on the head, coming down on the beard, even the beard of Aaron, coming down upon the edge of his [priestly] robes [consecrating the whole body]. It is like the dew of [Mount] Hermon coming down on the hills of Zion; for there the LORD has commanded the blessing: life forevermore. (Psalm 133 AMP)

Strife and division can stop the flow of the Spirit in our lives. It can also hinder our blessings. Strife is designed to destroy our lives, our relationships, and even the church. When it rises up against us and we do not actively resist it, it shuts us down. We must not fail to stand up to strife, or else the blessings that God has in store for us will be blocked. Anytime that we are about to see a breakthrough in our lives, the enemy will try to bring strife and division within our relationships, especially with our spouse. We must recognize the schemes and rebuke them.

Strife is defined as vigorous or bitter conflict, discord, antagonism, quarrel, struggle, or clash. It seeks to destroy us and block the flow of God's grace into our lives. It divides people and comes straight from the enemy, a thief who intends to kill, steal, and destroy the abundant life that God wants us to enjoy.

Strife destroys unity, creates division, causes confusion, and opens the door for "every evil work," according to James 3:16. Strife is the opposite of love. When people get into strife, they get out of love. Love is the antidote for sin and the foundation of the spiritual power we have as believers. If we allow strife in our lives, we nullify the power of love in our lives. We effectively shut down strife and render Satan defenseless when we begin walking in love. Love covers a multitude of sins (1 Peter 4:8).

> Above all, have fervent and unfailing love for one another, because love covers a multitude of sins [it overlooks unkindness and unselfishly seeks the best for others]. (1 Peter 4:8 AMP)

To win the battle over strife, we must focus on the spiritual, not the physical. Remember that we are not fighting against flesh-and-blood enemies but against evil rulers and authorities of the unseen world, against mighty powers in this dark world and against evil spirits in the heavenly places (Ephesians 6:12). "The weapons of our warfare are not carnal but mighty in God for pulling down of strongholds" (2 Corinthians 10:4 NKJV). Strife is evil, and it creates this atmosphere of bickering, arguing, and all sorts of things that offend people. Strife is a trap the devil lays to destroy marriages, businesses, and even churches.

> But if you have bitter jealousy and selfish ambition in your hearts, do not be arrogant, and [as a result] be in defiance of the truth. This [superficial] wisdom is not that which comes down from above, but is earthly (secular), natural (unspiritual), even demonic. For where jealousy and selfish ambition exist, there is disorder [unrest, rebellion] and every evil thing and morally degrading practice. James 3:14–16 (AMP)

Pride and selfishness are the root causes of strife. Anytime that you see strife, you can trace it back to pride. Envy and selfish ambition will also open the door to strife. We must recognize what is causing the quarrels among us. Is it pride, selfishness, or envy/jealousy?

> By pride comes nothing but strife, but with the well-advised is wisdom. (Proverbs 13:10 NKJV)

> What leads to [the unending] quarrels and conflicts among you? Do they not come from your [hedonistic]

desires that wage war in your [bodily] members [fighting for control over you]? You are jealous and covet [what others have] and your lust goes unfulfilled; so you murder. You are envious and cannot obtain [the object of your envy]; so you fight and battle. You do not have because you do not ask [it of God]. You ask [God for something] and do not receive it, because you ask with wrong motives [out of selfishness or with an unrighteous agenda], so that [when you get what you want] you may spend it on your [hedonistic] desires. (James 4:1–3 AMP)

It is God's will for us to live in peace and harmony with one another. 1 Peter 3:11 (AMP) says, "He must search for peace (with God, with self, with others) and pursue it eagerly (actively–not merely desiring it)." When the opportunity for strife arises, choose to be at peace. Forgive and walk in love. Hatred stirs up strife, but love covers and overwhelms all transgressions (Proverbs 10:12).

Hatred stirs up strife, but love covers and overwhelms all transgressions [forgiving and overlooking another's faults]. (Proverbs 10:12 AMP)

Having peace with others does not mean we won't ever disagree, but we must do it respectfully to avoid strife. We must seek unity and peace in our marriage and relationships, knowing that is the place of the Lord's Spirit dwelling and blessing. If you keep bringing up pain from the past, you are going to have strife in the present. You may be right about what happened, but do you want to be right, or do you want to have peace in your relationship? So many people do not even have peace within themselves, and therefore they can't be at peace with others. You can't be a peacemaker if you don't have peace yourself. Jesus is our peace. He is Jehovah Shalom—the Lord is peace. It is only when we abide in Him that we can have perfect peace. You cannot have peace without Jesus.

You will keep in perfect and constant peace the one whose mind is steadfast [that is, committed and focused on You—in both inclination and character], because he trusts and takes refuge in You [with hope and confident expectation]. (Isaiah 26:3 AMP)

Peace I leave with you; My [perfect] peace I give to you; not as the world gives do I give to you. Do not let your heart be troubled, nor let it be afraid. [Let My perfect peace calm you in every circumstance and give you courage and strength for every challenge.] (John 14:27 AMP)

Pastor Bill Johnson said, "You only have authority over the storm that you can sleep in." Jesus was at perfect peace and was sleeping through the storm while His disciples were freaking out (read the story in Mark 4:35–41 NKJV). The disciples woke Jesus and said to him, "Teacher, do You not care that we are perishing?" Then He arose and rebuked the wind and said to the sea, "Peace, be still!" And the wind ceased and there was a great calm. Only the peace of Jesus can calm us in every circumstance and storm. "Peace is not the absence of trouble but the presence of Christ." - Sheila Walsh

When you have peace within yourself, only then can you have peace within your relationships. When I finally found the peace of God, I never wanted to go a day without it. Whenever something gets me out of peace, I will go spend time with the Lord until I have peace again.

To have unity and agreement in our relationships, we need peace. It is a choice that we all have each day—whether or not we will seek the peace of Jesus. We can choose to let the storms get inside of us, or we can say, "Not today, Satan." We can choose to let disagreements lead to strife and chaos, or we can choose to resolve them in a healthy way. Too many people have been robbed of God's blessings and relationships because of strife. Be determined to avoid strife and let the fruit and power of God's Spirit flow through your life.

I once heard my pastor (Darrell Sutton) say, "You can't go east and west at the same time." He was referring to walking in sin and walking with Jesus. You cannot do both at the same time. I even think that the same goes for our relationships. You cannot have one spouse walking east and the other walking west at the same time. Well, physically you can, but you know what I am saying. When we are not in agreement and we are divided, it is not going to go well for us. If a house is divided against itself, that house will not be able to stand (Mark 3:25). When we enter into a covenant of marriage, the two become one. Satan works to divide the one back into two. We must fight for unity and peace in our marriage.

> And if a house is divided against itself, that house cannot stand. (Mark 3:25 AMP)

I think the hardest part for me as I was getting mentored and was growing and changing was being patient with my husband since he did not have a mentor or anyone speaking the truth into him. When I tried to speak the truth to my husband, it was usually not received and ended up in a quarrel. I had to trust that as God was changing me, He would also change my husband. I spoke less and spent more time in prayer, asking the Lord to send godly men to my husband's life so that he could receive their wisdom. I also found that by sharing what I was learning and how I was growing would inspire him to want to change for the better. I will admit that I was fearful that I would keep growing but my husband would stay the same, thinking that he did not have to change. As I surrendered those fears to the Lord, God answered my prayers, and somehow my husband started growing and changing along with me. God is faithful! He never just gets a hold of one person in a family. You better believe that if He can get one heart turned to Him, He will be faithful to turn the other hearts in the family, no matter how long it takes. Just be patient and persistent in prayer. Allow God to do the work in you, and He will work in your spouse.

It is so important to support one another and be a team in your marriage, parenting, finances, ministry, etc. Pray together, dream together, and do life together. Work toward common goals. Use the gifts that God has given you to work together for His glory. Do you know that you and your spouse have the right combination of spiritual gifts that go together, like peas and carrots, to build God's kingdom and bring Him glory? Find out what your spiritual gifts are. Take a spiritual gifts test online and find out more about each other. You will most likely see that you are exact opposites because opposites attract. If you were married to someone just like you, you would clash all the time and drive each other bonkers! God put you together for a reason. Your gifts, talents, and personalities help you balance each other out. Appreciate your differences and work together to carry out the purposes that God has for your lives. Do not allow the enemy to tear you apart anymore. Get into agreement with each other and work toward fulfilling the purposes of God. One of my favorite verses in the Bible is Acts 13:36. It says that David served the purposes of God in his own generation. Let that be your prayer for you and your spouse—that you would serve the purposes of God together in your generation.

> For David, after he had served the purpose of God in his own generation, fell asleep and was buried among his fathers and experienced decay [in the grave]. (Acts 13:36 AMP)

Summary

- Unity is where the Spirit dwells. That is the place where the Lord releases His blessings.
- Strife is defined as vigorous or bitter conflict, discord, or antagonism; a quarrel, struggle, or clash. It seeks to destroy us and block the flow of God's grace into our lives.
- It is God's will for us to live in peace and harmony with one another.
- Having peace with others does not mean we won't ever disagree, but we must do it respectfully and avoid strife.
- Jesus is our peace. He is Jehovah Shalom—the Lord is peace. It is only when we abide in Him that we can have perfect peace.
- When you have peace within yourself, only then can you have peace within your relationships.
- When we are not in agreement and are divided, it is not going to go well for us. If a house is divided against itself, that house will not be able to stand (Mark 3:25).

Questions

1. How is the Holy Spirit speaking to me through this chapter?

2. Is our marriage one of strife or one of unity? If there is strife in our marriage, how can we deal with it? How can we come together in unity?

3. Is there peace in our marriage? Is there peace within my heart? What can I do to ensure that I am at peace every day? What do I need to do the moment that I lose my peace?

4. Do my spouse and I support each other? Are we working together as a team? How can we work together to fulfill God's purpose for our lives?

Prayer

Heavenly Father, please forgive us when we have walked in disunity and strife. Help us to walk in peace, unity, and love with one another. I pray that we will work together to serve the purposes of God and bring You honor and glory in Jesus's name. Amen.

CHAPTER 20

The Joining of Two Families

For this reason a man shall leave his father and his mother, and shall be joined to his wife; and they shall become one flesh.
—Genesis 2:24 (AMP)

You have probably heard the saying, "When you marry someone, you marry their entire family." While it is true to say that you marry into the spouse's family, I believe it is wrong to say that you "marry" your spouse's family. Genesis 2:24 tells us that marriage involves leaving your mother and father and cleaving to each other, not each other's mother and father. The Bible never says that six people become one flesh; only two people become one flesh.

When we enter a covenant of marriage, we enter a oneness where the two become one flesh. Oneness in marriage reaches far beyond the physical level. The biblical view of "one flesh" communicates a unity that covers every facet of a couple's joint lives as husband and wife. In marriage, two whole lives unite together as one emotionally, intellectually, financially, spiritually, and in every other way. The "two shall become one" in purpose. They are so close that they function like one person, balancing each other's strengths and weaknesses so that together they can fulfill their God-given calling.

In joining your two lives together, there is no way to get out of the reality that you and your spouse's family history will have an impact on your relationship. It matters whether you and your spouse grew up in a loving home or a harsh one, a broken home or a whole one. While there is no such thing as a perfect family, it does matter how you were raised and whether you grew up in a good or a toxic environment. It matters how your parents chose to parent, and it matters how your character was formed when you were a child. If there are things that you each do not like about the way that you and your family or your spouse and his family treat one another, you'll want to discuss it because it's almost guaranteed to come up in your married life together at some point.

You must also find healing from any abuse (physical, verbal, emotional, sexual) or neglect that you experienced as a child. When we have trauma as a child, if it is not dealt with and healed, it will affect us as adults. So many of the issues that we have as adults stem from unhealed childhood wounds and trauma. That does not mean that we can use it as an excuse to act out on others, but I'm saying that it will affect you and your relationships, and that is why it is so important to find healing. Hurt people hurt other people, but healed people heal other people. "If you don't heal from what hurt you, you will bleed on people who didn't cut you" - Unknown. Seek biblical counseling and continually go to Jesus, asking Him to help heal all your wounds. The key to being made whole is finding the One (Jesus Christ) who holds all things together (Colossians 1:17).

You can also have trauma from different events that happened in your life. Unresolved trauma affects the way we think, feel, and make decisions, as well as impacts our identity and physical health. Studies have shown a strong link between addictions and trauma. People who have addictions are trying to deal with the trauma that has happened in their lives and numb their pain. Trauma is real and needs to be dealt with and healed. If not, it will affect you and every relationship you have. Your healing matters because healed people see differently. Healed people think differently. They have a different perspective. If we are not healed, we will use yesterday's pain as today's perspective. The pain/trauma was not your fault, but the healing is your responsibility. You cannot help the pain/trauma that happened to you, but you can decide to find healing and freedom from it. If you have had trauma in your life, I encourage you to read *Supernatural Freedom from the Captivity of Trauma* by Dr. Mike Hutchings.

You and your spouse are different from your families, but you were each formed by your own family. The good news is that even though you both come from very different families, you can decide what you want your family to look like. Sometimes creating a healthy marriage means that you must unlearn the unhealthy patterns you inherited from your family. You do not have the ability to change where you came from, but you do have the ability to dictate exactly how you would like your own family unit to be. You can pick the traditions and expectations that you did like from each family and throw out the ones that you do not like. You can form your own family that has its own culture.

There are things that are "normal," or acceptable, in our own families that may rub our spouse the wrong way. Every family is different and has their own customs, practices, and traditions deeply embedded into them. You might not even be aware of them until your spouse points it out or you come into conflict with them. While you can do things differently in your own home with your own family, it is still important to respect the different cultures and traditions of your respective families. You may not agree with everything and you do not have to participate in all that the family does, but it is still important to honor them, even if you disagree.

Scripture tells us to honor our father and our mother and things will go well for us and we will have a long life (Exodus 20:12; Ephesians 6:2–3). This does not just mean our own father and mother, but it also means our in-laws. I know some of you are cringing while you are reading this. You may be thinking to yourself right now, *Well, you do not know how my mother, father, or in-laws act. How can I honor them when they act dishonorably?*

God never said that we are to honor because our parents act honorably or because they are right. Scripture tells us to honor them because they are our parents, and it is a commandment from the Lord. When we show them honor, things will go well for us. I believe one of the reasons that things do not go well for some people is because they dishonor their parents. When you slander, backbite, are bitter, or withhold forgiveness from your parents, you are not showing them honor. I know it can be hard. I am not saying it is easy because we won't agree with everything that our parents do, and some may have been hurt and wounded by their own parents. No parent is perfect. Your parents are not perfect. Your spouse's parents are not perfect. If you decide to have children, you and your spouse will not be perfect parents either. Even if you do not agree with anything that they do, you can still show them honor. You may have to set boundaries to protect yourself and your family, but you can still show honor. Ask the Lord what that looks like for you and your situation.

> Honor (respect, obey, care for) your father and your mother, so that your days may be prolonged in the land the LORD your God gives you. (Exodus 20:12 AMP)

> Honor [esteem, value as precious] your father and your mother [and be respectful to them]—this is the first commandment with a promise—so that it may be well with you, and that you may have a long life on the earth. (Ephesians 6:2–3 AMP)

I know that family dynamics can create tension and stress in your relationship, but you can work through it. You can discuss different issues that arise and find a solution, but you should not slander each other's families. Never talk bad about one another's parents. You are not only dishonoring them, you are also dishonoring your spouse and, most importantly, dishonoring the Lord. We will be held accountable for the words we speak and the way that we treat other people. Remember, what we sow, we will reap (Galatians 6:7).

> But I say to you that for every idle word men may speak, they will give account of it in the day of judgment. For by your words you will be justified, and by your words you will be condemned. (Matthew 12:36–37 NKJV)

I remember early on in our marriage, my husband and I had many fights because we parented so differently. We had come from two families that had completely different ways of doing things. We learned that you will either do what you have seen modeled for you, or you do the exact opposite because you did not agree with what your parents did. Many of our fights were regarding parenting. It was not until we really started growing in our relationship with Christ that things began to change for us. We had to sit down and talk about how we wanted to parent our children so that we could train them in the way that they should go (Proverbs 22:6) and be on the same page with each other. One parent will typically be stricter while the other one is more lenient.

We had to find a balance of working together. Sometimes when I was too harsh with the kids, my merciful husband would tell me that they just needed a hug. Then, when my husband would lose his patience and get upset with them, I would have to calm him down and encourage him to not react out of his flesh or to apologize for overreacting. When we found that balance together and started listening to each other, then we could better parent our children. Our two older boys will even tell you that they had BC (before Christ) and AC (after Christ) parents. It was not that we were bad parents—we were just doing the best that we knew how to do. But it is amazing the wisdom that the Holy Spirit gives you when you seek Him in how to parent your children. There is no cookie-cutter approach. What works for one child will not work for another. We have five children who are all so different and need to be loved and disciplined in different ways. Learning to rely upon the Holy Spirit to teach us and give us wisdom changed everything for us as parents.

> Train up a child in the way he should go [teaching him to seek
> God's wisdom and will for his abilities and talents], even when
> he is old he will not depart from it. (Proverbs 22:6 AMP)

One thing that my mentor taught me regarding parenting was to make it a teaching ground in our home, not a training ground. What she meant by this was to take every opportunity to teach our children why something was wrong, rather than just yelling at them for it. If you think of a military training ground, you can picture the drill sergeant screaming at the soldiers telling them to do this and do that. While that may be an effective approach for the military, it is not an effective way to parent your children. Children do not learn when we just scream at them, but they learn when we gently teach them. I have found that every time I have sought the Lord with how to handle a situation, He will give me the wisdom that I need to share with my child to teach them, and the result is always fruitful. So the next time that you want to yell at your child, I encourage you to step away and go seek the Lord on how to manage the situation. Pray, find a scripture, talk with your spouse, and ask God for wisdom. When we ask for wisdom, God will freely give it to us (James 1:5).

> If any of you lacks wisdom, let him ask of God, who gives
> to all liberally and without reproach, and it will be given
> to him. (James 1:5 NKJV)

When we seek the Lord for solutions to our problems, He will always deliver. So many times, I have sought Him in different situations with my spouse and children, and He always gives me the wisdom that I need to handle the situation. I remember one time being upset at my son for something he had done. I just wanted to ground him for it and take away all his privileges. I then heard the Lord say, "Show him mercy." I was like, "What? Are you kidding me?" But I realized that the Lord wanted me to show my son the same mercy that He has shown to me over and over. My son knew that he had done something wrong. Punishing him for what he did was only going to shame him and push him into a pit even more. God knew that he just needed to be extended mercy. I am so thankful that I listened and *responded* accordingly, rather than *reacting* out of my flesh.

Joyce Meyers says, "Let emotions subside before you decide." When you are upset about a certain situation, calm down first and let your emotions subside before you decide what to do. Never react out of anger for it will not go well. We can hurt and damage our spouse or children so much by reacting out of our emotions rather than responding the way that we should. No person will ever get every situation right, but when we do mess up and handle something incorrectly, the first thing to do is to admit it and repent.

When you approach a situation wrong and lash out at your spouse or child, humble yourself and repent. Humility and repentance speak volumes to others, especially our family. It also shows our children how to repent when they do something wrong. Their little hearts need to hear us say, "I am sorry that I hurt your heart. Will you please forgive me for acting the way that I did?" I have found that they are always so gracious and quick to forgive. It not only softens their hearts, it also softens our own hearts. God loves it when we walk in humility, not pride. God opposes the proud but gives grace to the humble (James 4:6).

> But He gives us more and more grace [through the power of the Holy Spirit to defy sin and live an obedient life that reflects both our faith and our gratitude for our salvation]. Therefore, it says, "God is opposed to the proud and haughty, but [continually] gives [the gift of] grace to the humble [who turn away from self-righteousness]." (James 4:6 AMP)

As you join your families together, I encourage you to seek the Lord. Only He knows what you and your family need and how it should function together as a whole. Only God can give you the wisdom and insight that you need each day. Only He can give us grace for each season and new mercies every morning. When we keep God first in our marriage and family, He will work everything out. God loves family. He created Adam and Eve and told them to be fruitful and multiply (Genesis 1:28).

Satan is the one that comes to steal, kill, and destroy (John 10:10) just like he did in the garden of Eden when he tempted Eve. The Bible says that the devil prowls around like a roaring lion, seeking someone to devour (1 Peter 5:8). The enemy hates God's children and families. His goal is to destroy marriages and families. Be alert and aware of the enemy's schemes. Fight for your marriage and your family. Get on your knees to pray every day for your spouse and family. There should not be a single day that your Heavenly Father doesn't hear you praying for your spouse or family. Plead the blood of Jesus over your marriage and children every day. Ask God to put a hedge of protection around you and everything connected to you. One of my favorite scriptures to pray is 2 Thessalonians 3:3 (NIV): "But the LORD is faithful, and he will strengthen you and protect you from the evil one." Prayer is how we fight our battles. Do not forget to begin each morning on your knees for your family. There is power in prayer! James 5:16 (NKJV) says, "The effective, fervent prayer of a righteous man avails much."

> Be sober [well balanced and self-disciplined], be alert and cautious at all times. That enemy of yours, the devil, prowls around like a roaring lion [fiercely hungry], seeking someone to devour. (1 Peter 5:8 AMP)

Summary

- Genesis 2:24 tells us that marriage involves leaving your mother and father and cleaving to each other, not each other's mother and father. The Bible never says that six people become one flesh; only two people become one flesh.
- In joining your two lives together, there is no way to get out of the reality that you and your spouse's family history will have an impact on your relationship.
- When we have trauma as a child, if it is not dealt with and healed, it will affect us as a grown adult. So many of the issues that we have as adults stem from unhealed childhood wounds and trauma.
- The pain/trauma was not your fault, but the healing is your responsibility. You cannot help what happened to you as a child, but you can decide to find healing and freedom from it.
- Learning to rely upon the Holy Spirit to teach us and give us wisdom can change everything for us as parents.
- When we keep God first in our marriage and family, He will work everything out.
- There should not be a single day that your Heavenly Father doesn't hear you praying for your spouse or family.

Questions

1. How is the Holy Spirit speaking to me through this chapter?

2. How have our families had an impact on our relationship? Are there unhealthy things that we learned that need to be unlearned? Are there any boundaries with family members that need to be put in place?

3. Is there any unhealed trauma from my childhood that needs to be dealt with? What steps can I take to find healing? Have I asked Jesus to heal my wounds?

4. Am I partnering with the Holy Spirit to help me as a spouse and a parent (if you have children)? Do I seek God for His wisdom? What scriptures am I relying upon?

Prayer

God, I thank You for the family that You have given to me. I ask that you bring healing to any pain or trauma that my spouse or I have experienced in our lives. Teach us how to be the spouse and parents that You want us to be. Give us wisdom on how to live our lives in a way that would honor You, in Jesus's name. Amen.

CHAPTER 21

Change One Thing

And we all, with unveiled face, continually seeing as in a mirror the glory of the Lord, are progressively being transformed into His image from [one degree of] glory to [even more] glory, which comes from the LORD, [who is] the Spirit.

—2 Corinthians 3:18 (AMP)

If you change nothing, then nothing will change. Albert Einstein said, "Insanity is doing the same thing over and over again and expecting different results." I think we can all relate to this in some areas of our lives. We have done the same thing over and over again and expected a different result. However, change begins with us first changing our minds, which then helps us change our words and actions. If you want to change your life, start by first changing and renewing your mind.

> And do not be conformed to this world [any longer with its superficial values and customs], but be transformed and progressively changed [as you mature spiritually] by the renewing of your mind [focusing on godly values and ethical attitudes], so that you may prove [for yourselves] what the will of God is, that which is good and acceptable and perfect [in His plan and purpose for you]. (Romans 12:2 AMP)

In order to change, we must learn God's truth and change the way that we think. The way you think determines the way you feel, and the way you feel determines the way you act. If you want to change the way you feel or act, start by changing the way you think. You can't just say that you need to love your spouse more. It is not going to work that way. You must change the way that you think about your spouse because that will change the way you feel, thus changing the way that you act. Ephesians 4:23 (NLT) says, "Let the Spirit renew your thoughts and attitudes." If you want to change anything in your behavior or anything in your emotions, you start with your thoughts and your attitude. Allow the Spirit to change your thoughts and attitudes, which will in turn change your actions and your life.

> Be continually renewed in the spirit of your mind [having a fresh, untarnished mental and spiritual attitude]. (Ephesians 4:23 AMP)

Our lives should constantly be evolving and changing for the good. As Christians, we should be continuously maturing and transforming into the image of Christ, from one degree of glory to even more glory (see 2 Corinthians 3:18), but we cannot do it on our own. If you try to change by your own self-will, it is not going to get you very far. We must surrender to the Lord and allow Him to change us. We apply His word to our lives and allow Him to work in and through us.

Every week when I would meet with my mentor, she would ask how God was working in me—what He was pointing His finger at in my heart. If we have a teachable spirit and allow God to mold us, then we can look within at whatever God is pointing to in our lives that needs to be addressed. It could be our bad attitude, pride, fear, lust, the way we are treating someone, the way we are handling money, offense, unforgiveness, bitterness, judgment, selfishness, a bad habit, a secret sin, anger, the way that we are parenting, or ways that we could be a better spouse, etc. The Lord will deal with whatever needs to be dealt with in our lives if we allow Him to. We should always be growing and changing, allowing God to work in any area of our lives. We will never arrive.

If you think you have arrived, then that just means you are blinded by pride, and that needs to be dealt with. We all have blind spots where we cannot see what needs to be changed in our own lives, but other people can. It is so important to have a few people that we can trust who can point out the blind spots in our lives so that we can continue to change and grow. We should always be growing and changing, becoming more like Christ, until the day Christ Jesus returns or calls us home. We are a continuous work in progress. Once we get freedom in one area, we then move on to the next area or graduate to another level, where we need more freedom. God's goal is to transform our character so we can reflect more of Him!

> I am convinced and confident of this very thing, that He who has begun a good work in you will [continue to] perfect and complete it until the day of Christ Jesus [the time of His return]. (Philippians 1:6 AMP)

I know it can be overwhelming when we think of all that needs to be changed in our lives or how far we have to go. I want to encourage you to celebrate what God has done in you and how far you have come. Do not look at all that needs to change. Start by changing one thing. Ask the Lord what He wants to deal with in your life and marriage right now. You may be thinking that it is one thing when God will lead you to a completely different area. Trust that God knows what is best. Deal with whatever He is putting His finger on in your heart at the moment. Change is a process. I liken it to an onion that has layers upon layers. Deal with the first layer, and then God will lead you to the next. Unfortunately, we cannot just snap our fingers and have everything change in one day. It will be a continual process of change.

God is the Potter, and we are the clay (Isaiah 64:8). This verse tells us that God is our Father and Creator, and we are the work of His hand. He shapes us and molds us according to His will and purpose. We are dependent on Him and should trust Him as the Potter knows what is best for the clay. Allow God, the Potter, to mold you into the beautiful person that He created you to be!

> Yet, O LORD, You are our Father; we are the clay, and You our Potter, and we all are the work of Your hand. (Isaiah 64:8 AMP)

You cannot force yourself or anyone else to change. It must be a voluntary decision. Sometimes you have to get sick and tired of being sick and tired of whatever issue you are dealing with in your life. I believe that when you finally make up your mind to change, submit to the process, and allow the Spirit of God to work in your life, that is when you will begin to see results. So what is it in your life or marriage that needs to change? What are you sick and tired of being sick and tired of? Surrender it to the Lord and ask for His help.

Summary

- If you change nothing, then nothing will change. Albert Einstein said, "Insanity is doing the same thing over and over again and expecting different results."
- Change begins with us first changing our minds, which then helps us change our words and actions. If you want to change your life, start by changing and renewing your mind.
- The way you think determines the way you feel, and the way you feel determines the way you act. If you want to change the way you feel or act, start by changing the way you think.

- You can't just say that you need to love your spouse more. It is not going to work that way. You must change the way that you think about your spouse because that will change the way you feel, thus changing the way that you act.
- As Christians, we should be continuously maturing and transforming into the image of Christ, from one degree of glory to even more glory (see 2 Corinthians 3:18), but we cannot do it on our own. We must surrender to the Lord and allow Him to change us.
- We are a continuous work in progress. Once we get freedom in one area, we then move on to the next area or graduate to another level where we need more freedom. God's goal is to transform our character so we can reflect more of Him!
- Start by changing one thing. Ask the Lord what He wants to deal with in your life and marriage right now.

Questions

1. How is the Holy Spirit speaking to me through this chapter?

2. What needs to be changed in our marriage? What is the *one* thing that God wants me to deal with?

3. In what area do I need to change my thinking? What scriptures can I rely on to help me?

4. What can we celebrate in our marriage right now? What is going well?

Prayer

God, help me and my spouse be humble and teachable. I pray that we will allow You to mold us and shape us into the people You want us to be. Show us the one thing that You want to deal with right now in our marriage and help us to yield to the process in Jesus's name. Amen.

CHAPTER 22

Never Give Up

Let us not grow weary or become discouraged in doing good, for at the proper time we will reap, if we do not give in.
—Galatians 6:9 (AMP)

I have learned that if the devil knows that you have any quit in you, he will push you right up to that point. Galatians 6:9 (AMP) says, "Let us not grow weary or become discouraged in doing good, for at the proper time we will reap, if we do not give in." Satan wants you to give up on your marriage. He wants you to quit. He will send one thing after the next to try to wear you out, to get you to believe that it is best to just quit.

I believe one of the greatest tactics of the enemy is to wear out the saints and cause us to give up. The devil wants you to quit. He does not want your marriage to last. He does not want you to be an encouraged Christian because then you would make a difference in God's kingdom. If he can keep you pressed down with his little thumb and discouraged, then he has you right where he wants you. We must realize that part of Satan's plan for end-time believers is to make us weary. Daniel 7:25 (AMP) gives a vivid description of a vision that the prophet Daniel received regarding the last days: "And he 'shall wear out the saints of the Most High."

But God wants you to be encouraged. Romans 8:37 (AMP) gives Christians this good news: "Yet amid all these things we are more than conquerors and gain a surpassing victory through Him who loved us." The phrase "more than conquerors" means that before trouble even starts, we already know who wins. We do not fight for victory; we fight from a stance of victory. Through Christ, we are already victorious.

Sometimes we can become so weary when it seems that there is trouble after trouble. Psalm 34:19 (NKJV) says, "Many are the afflictions of the righteous, but the Lord delivers him out of them all." This is a promise that I cling to when trouble and weariness come my way. When we encounter hardships in life or in our marriage, we must encourage ourselves in the Lord just like David did in the Bible. David had just returned home with his fighting men when he found that his hometown had been attacked while he was away. The Amalekites had made a raid on Ziklag. The town had been burned, and all the women and children had been taken, including David's two wives. Everyone was grieved over the situation and wept. The men then turned in anger against David, and they all wanted to stone him.

We are told in 1 Samuel 30:6 (NKJV), "And David was greatly distressed, for the people spoke of stoning him, because the soul of all the people was grieved, every man for his sons and his daughters. But David strengthened himself in the LORD his God." The story goes on to say in 1 Samuel 30:18–20

(NKJV), "So David recovered all that the Amalekites had carried away, and David rescued his two wives. And nothing of theirs was lacking, either small or great, sons or daughters, spoil, or anything which they had taken from them; David recovered all. Then David took all the flocks and herds they had driven before those other livestock, and said, 'This is David's spoil.'"

There is no better encouragement than the encouragement that comes from the Lord. He always knows exactly what we need at every moment. A while back, I was crying out to the Lord for Him to refresh me. I was battle-weary from a difficult season that I had been walking through, and I needed encouragement. While I was in prayer, I remembered the scripture in Proverbs 11:25 (NIV) that says, "A generous person will prosper; whoever refreshes others will be refreshed."

I started to pray and ask the Lord how I could encourage and refresh my husband and all my kids. I got a specific scripture for each one of them and sent them all encouraging texts or notes. What was I doing? I was refreshing others because I needed to be refreshed. I was planting a seed. Whenever you are in need, go plant a seed. If you need encouragement for yourself, then go encourage someone else. If you need prayer, go pray for someone that you know also needs prayer. If you need a financial breakthrough, then go give to someone else in need. I have learned that it is more blessed to give than to receive (Acts 20:35), so when I am giving to others, it takes my mind off myself and brings me joy!

After I had sent those encouraging texts and written those notes for my family that day, I then got a text from a friend asking how my week was going. I told her that I had had better weeks before, but it was all good. I did not say anything more. Shortly after, I received flowers from this friend with a note saying, "Look up, child."

I don't cry a lot, but at that moment, I lost it! God was so good to send someone to encourage and refresh me just when I needed it.

The best thing that you can do when you are battle-weary is go to the Lord in prayer and read His Word. Keep reading until God speaks to you through His Word. There are many ways that God speaks to us, but one of the best ways is through His Word. You will find the hope and encouragement that you need in His Word. Also, find a scripture(s) that you can pray specifically for your situation. There is power in praying God's Word, and it does not return void (see Isaiah 55:11). I love to read the Psalms when I am feeling discouraged and need to be encouraged. Read until God speaks to you.

> So will My word be which goes out of My mouth; it will not return to Me void (useless, without result), without accomplishing what I desire, and without succeeding in the matter for which I sent it. (Isaiah 55:11 AMP)

If you have felt like you got knocked down and lost your fight, I am telling you right now to *get back up!* Encourage yourself in the Lord and get your fight back! Get a holy anger against the enemy and go to war for your marriage and family. Rise up and tell the enemy that you are not going to quit and that he cannot have your marriage. You are not just fighting for yourself and your own marriage but also for your kingdom purposes together as a couple and for the generations to come. Do not let the enemy win. Rise up and fight! Fight the battles on your knees.

> So submit to [the authority of] God. Resist the devil [stand firm against him] and he will flee from you. (James 4:7 AMP)

Be persistent in prayer. In Luke 18, Jesus told his disciples a parable to show them that they should always pray and not give up. Luke 18:2–8 (NKJV) says, "There was in a certain city a judge who did not fear God nor regard man. Now there was a widow in that city; and she came to him, saying, "Get justice for me from my adversary." And he would not for a while; but afterward, he said within himself, "Though I do not fear God nor regard man, yet because this widow troubles me I will avenge her, lest by her continual coming she weary me." Then the LORD said, "Hear what the unjust judge said. And shall God not avenge His own elect who cry out day and night to Him, though He bears long with them? I tell you that He will avenge them speedily. Nevertheless, when the Son of Man comes, will He really find faith on the earth?"

Be like the persistent widow when it comes to praying for your marriage and do not ever give up. God is for your marriage; He will help you if you come to Him and ask. God hates divorce (see Malachi 2:16 NKJV), and for good reason. It can be devastating for all involved, and the negative effects can last for years. Divorce should always be a last resort. But God does allow for divorce in some cases when marriage vows are broken. I'm not in any way promoting divorce, but I know that the Old Testament allows for, and the New Testament affirms, the following grounds for divorce: adultery (Deuteronomy 24:1, affirmed by Jesus in Matthew 19), emotional and physical neglect (Exodus 21:10–11, affirmed by Paul in 1 Corinthians 7), or abandonment (as affirmed in 1 Corinthians 7:15).

> When a man takes a wife and marries her, and it happens that she finds no favor in his eyes because he has found some uncleanness in her, and he writes her a certificate of divorce, puts it in her hand, and sends her out of his house. (Deuteronomy 24:1 NKJV)

Marriage and Divorce

Now it came to pass, when Jesus had finished these sayings, that He departed from Galilee and came to the region of Judea beyond the Jordan. And great multitudes followed Him, and He healed them there. The Pharisees also came to Him, testing Him, and saying to Him, "Is it lawful for a man to divorce his wife for just any reason?" And He answered and said to them, "Have you not read that He who made them at the beginning 'made them male and female,' and said, 'For this reason a man shall leave his father and mother and be joined to his wife, and the two shall become one flesh'? So then, they are no longer two but one flesh. Therefore, what God has joined together, let not man separate." They said to Him, "Why then did Moses command to give a certificate of divorce, and to put her away?" He said to them, "Moses, because of the hardness of your hearts, permitted you to divorce your wives, but from the beginning it was not so. And I say to you, whoever divorces his wife, except for sexual immorality, and marries another, commits adultery; and whoever marries her who is divorced commits adultery." His disciples said to Him, "If such is the case of the man with his wife, it is better not to marry." But He said to them, "All cannot accept this saying, but only those to whom it has been given: For there are eunuchs who were born thus from their mother's womb, and there are eunuchs who were made eunuchs by men, and there are eunuchs who have made themselves eunuchs for the kingdom of heaven's sake. He who is able to accept it, let him accept it." (Matthew 19:1–12 NKJV)

If he takes another wife, he shall not diminish her food, her clothing, and her marriage rights. And if he does not do these three for her, then she shall go out free, without paying money. (Exodus 21:10–11 NKJV)

Now to the married I command, yet not I but the LORD: A wife is not to depart from her husband. But even if she does depart, let her remain unmarried or be reconciled to her husband. And a husband is not to divorce his wife. But to the rest I, not the LORD, say: If any brother has a wife who does not believe, and she is willing to live with him, let him not divorce her. And a woman who has a husband who does not believe, if he is willing to live with her, let her not divorce him. For the unbelieving husband is sanctified by the wife, and the unbelieving wife is sanctified by the husband; otherwise your children would be unclean, but now they are holy. But if the unbeliever departs, let him depart; a brother or a sister is not under bondage in such cases. But God has called us to peace. For how do you know, O wife, whether you will save your husband? Or how do you know, O husband, whether you will save your wife? (1 Corinthians 7:10–16 NKJV)

A wife is bound by law as long as her husband lives; but if her husband dies, she is at liberty to be married to whom she wishes, only in the LORD. (1 Corinthians 7:39 NKJV)

If you have gone through a divorce, I am so sorry, and please know that I am not condemning you in any way. "There is therefore now no condemnation to those who are in Christ Jesus, who do not walk according to the flesh, but according to the Spirit" (Romans 8:1 NKJV). I know of many couples where one spouse did not want a divorce and tried everything they could to save their marriage, but the other one did, and there was nothing that they could do to change it. I know of other marriages where the spouse did not want the divorce but due to infidelity and abuse, it was in their best interest to leave in order to protect themselves. I also know of marriages where there was infidelity, but through confession, repentance, and forgiveness, God restored their marriage. Every marriage situation is different. I don't know your story, but God does. He is the One who knows all and sees all. He loves you no matter what.

Marriage is not easy. If it were easy, the divorce rate would not be so high. It takes time, selflessness, effort, patience, love, forgiveness, and a whole lot of grace. I want to encourage you. Whatever you do, *don't give up!* Nothing is impossible with God (Luke 1:37). Love always trusts, always hopes, and always perseveres (1 Corinthians 13:7). Love never fails (1 Corinthians 13:8). Surrender your marriage to God and watch Him work. "Therefore, what God has joined together, let not man separate" (Mark 10:9 NKJV).

> Love suffers long and is kind; love does not envy; love does not parade itself, is not puffed up; does not behave rudely, does not seek its own, is not provoked, thinks no evil; does not rejoice in iniquity, but rejoices in the truth; bears all things, believes all things, hopes all things, endures all things. Love never fails. But whether there are prophecies, they will fail; whether there are tongues, they will cease; whether there is knowledge, it will vanish away. (1 Corinthians 13:4–8 NKJV)

Summary

- I have learned that if the devil knows that you have any quit in you, he will push you right up to that point.
- Satan wants you to give up on your marriage. He wants you to quit. He will send one thing after the next to try to wear you out, to get you to believe that it is best to just quit.

- When we encounter hardships in life or in our marriages, we must encourage ourselves in the Lord just like David did in the Bible.
- There is no better encouragement than the encouragement that comes from the Lord. He always knows exactly what we need at every moment.
- Find a scripture(s) that you can pray specifically for your situation. There is power in praying God's Word, and it does not return void (see Isaiah 55:11).
- If you have felt like you got knocked down and lost your fight, I am telling you right now: *Get back up!*
- You are not just fighting for yourself and your own marriage but also for your kingdom purposes together as a couple and for the generations to come. Do not let the enemy win. Rise up and fight! Fight the battles on your knees.

Questions

1. How is the Holy Spirit speaking to me through this chapter?

2. How can I encourage myself in the Lord when I feel like giving up? What scriptures can I stand on?

3. What scriptures can I pray for our marriage? Am I being persistent in praying for our marriage?

4. What can we do together to ensure that our marriage stays strong?

Prayer

God, I thank You that You are for our marriage. What You have joined together, let no man separate. Help us to not give up but to fight for our marriage. I pray that You will restore anything that has been broken. Help us work together to create the marriage that You have designed for us to have. May our marriage become a reflection of You, in Jesus's name. Amen.

CHAPTER 23

Renew

Therefore if anyone is in Christ [that is, grafted in, joined to Him by faith in Him as Savior], he is a new creature [reborn and renewed by the Holy Spirit]; the old things [the previous moral and spiritual condition] have passed away. Behold, new things have come [because spiritual awakening brings a new life].

—2 Corinthians 5:17 (AMP)

If you are in Christ—that is, you have received Christ as your Lord and Savior—then you are a born-again new creation. The old things (your previous moral and spiritual condition) have passed away, and the new things have come (because a spiritual awakening brings new life). When God saves us, he not only washes all our sins away, but He joins us to Christ. He makes us one with Christ. Our lives are no longer worldly—they are now spiritual. Our "death" to the old sin nature was nailed to the cross with Christ. It was buried with Him, and just as He was raised up by the Father, so are we raised up to "walk in newness of life" (see Romans 6:4).

> We have therefore been buried with Him through baptism into death, so that just as Christ was raised from the dead through the glory and power of the Father, we too might walk habitually in newness of life [abandoning our old ways]. (Romans 6:4 AMP)

When we receive Christ as our Savior, we exchange our old life for a new one. We exchange sin for forgiveness, pride for humility, legalism for grace, fear for love, weakness for strength, and anger for joy. Once we surrender our lives to God, He sends His Holy Spirit to dwell within us to begin a process of transformation and sanctification. It is a daily process to which we must yield.

Sin is natural for the unbeliever. Just like taking a breath, it is not even something they think about. But after receiving Christ and having the Holy Spirit live within you, there is now a moral compass that convicts and leads you. It is no longer natural for you to sin. When we do sin, that inner alarm goes off, and we are expected to do something about it. In other words, habitual sin is no longer a choice for us. In 1 John 3:9 (NKJV), we are told, "Whoever has been born of God does not sin, for His seed remains in him; and he cannot sin, because he has been born of God."

If you are continuing to commit the same old sins, day in and day out, something is terribly wrong. Habitual sin is the evidence of rebellion, and rebellion will affect the quality of your relationship with Christ. Paul realized that when he said in Romans 6:1–2 (ESV), "What shall we say then? Are we to continue in sin that grace may abound? By no means! How can we who died to sin still live in it?"

If we are truly walking with Jesus each day, we will not be walking in habitual sin. We will still sin occasionally and fall short of the glory of God just as the Bible says in Romans 3:23, because none of us are perfect, and no one will ever be. But when we do sin, we will want to repent and turn from it; we will not continue walking in that same sin. There is freedom in Christ when we walk with Him daily.

> It was for this freedom that Christ set us free [completely liberating us]; therefore keep standing firm and do not be subject again to a yoke of slavery [which you once removed]. (Galatians 5:1 AMP)

We need Jesus in our lives. Our marriages need Jesus. We cannot have the marriage that we desire apart from Him. Your marriage is to be a reflection of Christ and the church. The relationship that God set up between Jesus Christ and His church (us, His people) is the marriage relationship. God beautifully paints the marriage portrait of Christ as the groom and us as His bride. Marriage is to be a mirror image of Christ's love for His people, loving and serving each other unconditionally, dying to selfishness, building the other one up, all to point others to Christ.

Marriage Like Christ and the Church

> Wives, be subject to your own husbands, as [a service] to the LORD. For the husband is head of the wife, as Christ is head of the church, Himself being the Savior of the body. But as the church is subject to Christ, so also wives should be subject to their husbands in everything [respecting both their position as protector and their responsibility to God as head of the house]. Husbands, love your wives [seek the highest good for her and surround her with a caring, unselfish love], just as Christ also loved the church and gave Himself up for her, so that He might sanctify the church, having cleansed her by the washing of water with the word [of God], so that [in turn] He might present the church to Himself in glorious splendor, without spot or

wrinkle or any such thing; but that she would be holy [set apart for God] and blameless. Even so husbands should and are morally obligated to love their own wives as [being in a sense] their own bodies. He who loves his own wife loves himself. For no one ever hated his own body, but [instead] he nourishes and protects and cherishes it, just as Christ does the church, because we are members (parts) of His body. For this reason, a man shall leave his father and his mother and shall be joined [and be faithfully devoted] to his wife, and the two shall become one flesh. This mystery [of two becoming one] is great; but I am speaking with reference to [the relationship of] Christ and the church. However, each man among you [without exception] is to love his wife as his very own self [with behavior worthy of respect and esteem, always seeking the best for her with an attitude of lovingkindness], and the wife [must see to it] that she respects and delights in her husband [that she notices him and prefers him and treats him with loving concern, treasuring him, honoring him, and holding him dear]. (Ephesians 5:22–33 AMP)

As Christians, we are called to look like Christ in all that we say and do. Many of us forget that this also applies to our marriages. None of us are married to the perfect man or woman. Marriages take a lot of hard work. If marriages are meant to portray the picture that Christ has for His church, is it any surprise that Satan does all that he can to destroy it and tear us apart? We must fight for our marriages and not allow the enemy to destroy them.

Some of you need to put the past behind you and forgive so you can move forward. When the enemy tried to destroy a good friendship of mine, my friend and I met to talk about what had happened over the past couple of years. At the beginning of the conversation, I asked the question, "Where do we start?" She replied, "White as snow." We agreed to put all the offenses and things that had happened behind us, forgive each other, and move forward with a fresh, new start in our friendship. The best way to destroy any relationship is to hang on to any little offense and hold unforgiveness and bitterness in your heart. If you do this, you will not have healthy relationships. Learn to let go of the things that happened yesterday, a month, a year, or ten years ago. Forgive so that you *can* move forward into all that God has in store for you.

Sometimes we just need a fresh start in our marriage. A vow renewal is an effective way to reaffirm your commitment to one another. For couples who have had significant relational challenges, a vow renewal is a good way to mark a new beginning. For others who have been married for any amount of time, it is an effective way to renew and refresh the relationship and to be reminded of the reason you said, "I do."

To have a growing, healthy marriage, there must be a heart transformation. You won't have any lasting change with just head knowledge. There must be that connection between the head and the heart, which will produce the change you desire to see. Give your hearts and marriage to God and watch Him create something beautiful. Only He can give you beauty for ashes (Isaiah 61:3).

One thing that my husband and I do at the end of every year is go on a little getaway together. Since we have younger kids, we usually just make it a day trip. We take a short trip out of town, go out to eat at a nice restaurant, and sit down to reflect and dream together. It is always so good to look back on the year, to celebrate, and to see what changes need to be made in our lives. Then we like to look ahead and see what God wants to do in our future. We set goals together and share what we desire for the upcoming year. We pray and ask God what He wants to do in and through our marriage, our family, ministry, and businesses. It is always such a good way to end the year and begin a new one!

New beginnings are always good. Nobody ever complains about new beginnings. There is such a freshness, excitement, and energy in starting new things. I want to encourage a new beginning for your marriage. Maybe you have a wonderful marriage and don't think that it needs to be any better. I am so happy for you, and we celebrate your marriage. I do believe that our marriages can always be better and that they should always be growing so they do not stagnate. Think of an Olympic athlete: They never reach a point where they think they do not have to improve. No, they are constantly training and being coached by others, so that they can continue to improve and be the best that they can possibly be. Even when they are the best in the world, they are still working to become better. We should be the same. Good should never be good enough. There is always a new level that we can go to in our relationship with Christ and our relationship with our spouse. If we are not learning and growing, then we are not changing. God wants to transform us from glory to glory (2 Corinthians 3:18)—in other words, from a current glorious place to another higher glorious place. Allow the Lord to continue to transform you from one degree of glory to even more glory.

> And we all, with unveiled face, continually seeing as in a mirror the glory of the LORD, are progressively being transformed into His image from [one degree of] glory to [even more] glory, which comes from the LORD, [who is] the Spirit. (2 Corinthians 3:18 AMP)

The word *renew* can be defined as "changing into something new and different, something better." If we are honest, I think we can all say that we would like our marriage to be better. Let's make the decision today to renew our marriages and allow God to have his way in our relationship with Him and with our spouses. After all, a marriage is not a final destination—it's a lifetime of love. Take the time to recommit your marriage to God and to one another.

I pray that this book inspired, challenged, and encouraged you. I hope that you were able to take away many nuggets of truth to apply to your own marriage. There is no cookie-cutter approach. Every marriage is different and has its own struggles, but I can tell you that when we do things God's way, it works. Even if nothing I wrote resonated with you, read the scriptures on marriage, and apply those to your lives. When you plant God's Word, you will see a harvest. His Word works! I pray that this book will help your marriage to not just survive but to thrive. We are cheering you on and praying for each one of you who reads this book. I know that it was not a coincidence that you read it. It was written for such a time as this in your life. God has good plans for you (Jeremiah 29:11) and for your marriage. May you be blessed!

> "For I know the plans and thoughts that I have for you," says the Lord, "plans for peace and well-being and not for disaster, to give you a future and a hope." (Jeremiah 29:11 AMP)

Our Prayer for Your Marriage

Heavenly Father, we thank You for the gift of marriage. We pray for every married couple who completes this book. We pray that You would sanctify and renew their covenant of marriage. Teach them Your ways, Lord, and help them walk in them so they can fulfill the biblical roles of husband and wife. We pray, God, that they will keep You first in their lives and in their marriage. Protect them from the schemes of the enemy. Help them to shut any open doors in their marriage where Satan has had an advantage. Bless them and keep them. What You joined together, let no man separate, in Jesus's name. Amen.

Eric and Amber Cunningham

Summary

- We need Jesus in our lives. Our marriage needs Jesus. We cannot have the marriage that we desire apart from Him.
- Marriage is to be a mirror image of Christ's love for His people, loving and serving each other unconditionally, dying to selfishness, building the other one up, all to point others to Christ.
- If a marriage is meant to portray the picture that Christ has for His church, is it any surprise that Satan does all that he can to destroy it and tear us apart? We must fight for our marriages and not allow the enemy to destroy them.
- The best way to destroy any relationship is to hang on to any little offense and hold unforgiveness and bitterness in your heart.
- Learn to let go of the things that happened yesterday, a month, a year, or ten years ago. Forgive so that you *can* move forward into all that God has for you.
- To have a growing, healthy marriage, there must be a heart transformation. You will not have any lasting change with just head knowledge. There must be that connection between the head and the heart, which will produce the change you desire to see.
- Every marriage is different and has its own struggles, but I can tell you that when we do things God's way, it works.

Questions

1. How is the Holy Spirit speaking to me through this chapter?

2. Is Jesus at the center of our marriage? Is our marriage a reflection of Christ's love? Do we selflessly serve and love one another? How can we love and serve each other more like Jesus?

3. Is there any hurt or offense that I need to let go of? What heart transformation needs to take place in me and my spouse?

4. Are we truly ready to leave the past behind and move forward into all that God has for our marriage? Are we ready, as a couple, to do things God's way? What steps can we take to create a new beginning?

Prayer

God, I thank You that You created marriage and that it is to reflect Christ and your church. I pray that You will bless our marriage and help us to become the spouses that You desire us to be. We yield our marriage to You and ask for You to have Your way. Renew our marriage today and help us honor You with this covenant that we made with You and with one another in Jesus's name. Amen.

TESTIMONIES

We would love to hear your feedback/testimony of how this book impacted you and your marriage. If you have a testimony that you would like to share with us, please email at howtotrainyourspouse@gmail.com. We pray that the tests you have gone through will become a testimony and that any mess in your marriage will become your message. May God use your story to witness to others and make an impact in lives, all for His glory!

VOW RENEWAL

Husband

I, _____, receive you, _____, as a gift from the hand of God and now reaffirm my love for you as my lifelong partner in marriage. I promise to love, honor, and cherish you from this day forward, in sickness and in health, for richer or poorer, for better or worse, and forsaking all others, to be faithful to you for as long as we both shall live.

Wife

I, _____, receive you, _____, as a gift from the hand of God and now reaffirm my love for you as my lifelong partner in marriage. I promise to love, honor, and cherish you from this day forward, in sickness and in health, for richer or poorer, for better or worse, and forsaking all others, to be faithful to you for as long as we both shall live.

Date _____   **Signed** _____

Printed in the United States
by Baker & Taylor Publisher Services